IN OLD PHOT

BRITA

WORDSLEY

PAST & PRESENT

STAN HILL

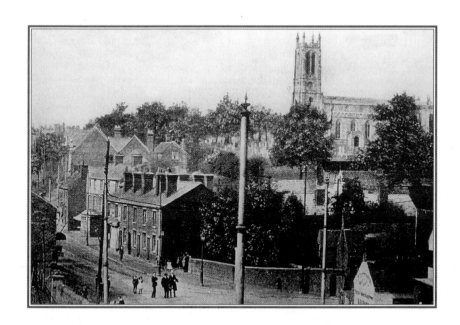

SUTTON PUBLISHING

Sutton Publishing Limited
Phoenix Mill · Thrupp · Stroud
Gloucestershire · GL5 2BU

First published 2005

Title page photograph: The bottom of High
Street before the First World War.

British Library Cataloguing in Publication Data
A catalogue record for this book is available from the
British Library.

ISBN 0-7509-3045-4

Typeset in 10.5/13.5 Photina.
Typesetting and origination by
Sutton Publishing Limited.
Printed and bound in England by
J.H. Haynes & Co. Ltd, Sparkford.

THE BLACK COUNTRY SOCIETY

The Black Country Society is proud to be associated with
Sutton Publishing of Stroud. In 1994 the society was
invited by Sutton Publishing to collaborate in what has
proved to be a highly successful publishing partnership,
namely the extension of the *Britain in Old Photographs*
series into the Black Country. In this joint venture the Black
Country Society has played an important role in establishing and developing a
major contribution to the region's photographic archives by encouraging society
members to compile books of photographs of the area or town in which they live.

The first book in the Black Country series was *Wednesbury in Old Photographs* by
Ian Bott, launched by Lord Archer of Sandwell in November 1994. Since then 65
Black Country titles have been published. The total number of photographs
contained in these books is in excess of 13,000, suggesting that the whole
collection is probably the largest regional photographic survey of its type in any
part of the country to date.

This voluntary society was founded in 1967 as a reaction to the trends of the
late 1950s and early '60s. This was a time when the reorganisation of local
government was seen as a threat to the identity of individual communities and
when, in the name of progress and modernisation, the industrial heritage of the
Black Country was in danger of being swept away.

The general aims of the society are to stimulate interest in the past, present and
future of the Black Country, and to secure at regional and national levels an
accurate understanding and portrayal of what constitutes the Black Country and,
wherever possible, to encourage and facilitate the preservation of the Black
Country's heritage.

The society, which now has over 2,500 members worldwide, organises a yearly
programme of activities. There are five venues in the Black Country where evening
meetings are held on a monthly basis from September to April. In the summer
months, there are fortnightly guided evening walks in the Black Country and its
green borderland, and there is also a full programme of excursions further afield by
car. Details of all these activities are to be found on the society's website,
www.blackcountrysociety.co.uk, and in *The Blackcountryman*, the quarterly
magazine that is distributed to all members.

PO Box 71 · Kingswinford · West Midlands DY6 9YN

CONTENTS

ACKNOWLEDGEMENTS

I should like to express special thanks to Fred Willetts and Wordsley History Society for their great contribution, Graham Beckley LBIPP for photographs and work on old photographs, Mrs Patricia Devall for word processing, A. Norman Piddock for photographs and access to property deeds relating to Greenbank.

For their contribution, either in photographs, information or both, I thank Eileen Bailey, Barbara Beadman, John Bradley, A. Blake Bromley, Bob Cotton, David J. Cox, John Dallaway, Roger Dodsworth, Angus Dunphy OBE, David Eades, C.J.L. Elwell OBE, Christopher Firmstone, Iris Gill, Mr and Mrs G.P. Gregg, Kevin Gripton, H. Jack Haden, Charles Hajdamach, Mike Harris, Mrs D.L. Hayes, Geoff Hill MBE, Mr V. Khadun, John Massey, Robert Oldnall for access to his late father's postcard collection, Edric Pearson, Malcolm Penn, Alan Pilkington, Gerald Potter, Frank Power, Ron Price, Barry Randle, John V. Richards, W. Eric Richardson, Jack Roberts, John Sanders, Mary Skidmore, Ian M. Stuart, Patrick Talbot, Pearl Taylor, Geoff Warburton, Trevor Worton, Susan Wright, Catherine Wood, George Wood, Lydia Yardley.

Thanks are also due to Aerofilms, the *Black Country Bugle*, the Black Country Society, Broadfield House Glass Museum, Stourbridge Library, the *Stourbridge News Incorporating County Express*, Tudor Crystal, the *Wolverhampton Express & Star*.

Sincere apologies for any omissions.

All royalties from the book will be donated to Mary Stevens Hospice, Stourbridge.

INTRODUCTION

The *Oxford Dictionary of Place Names* by A.D. Mills suggests that the name Wordsley comes from Wuluardesley, which is Old English (from the twelfth century) and means a woodland clearing belonging to a man named Wulfweard. The present spelling has been in use since the early eighteenth century.

Wordsley was part of the ancient Parish of Kingswinford, which had been virtually unchanged as a unit of ecclesiastical administration for nearly 1,000 years. The original Wordsley settlement in medieval times was probably around The Green, and there would have been scattered farmsteads. St Mary's Church was situated near the northern boundary of the large Kingswinford parish, where there had been a church since the Norman Conquest, and probably even before that. It was inconveniently situated to serve the growing villages over the 11 square miles of the parish, which extended over The Briar Hill to the River Stour, the Staffordshire/Worcestershire county boundary at the foot of Quarry Bank.

An important factor in the development of Wordsley was the road from Stourbridge to Kingswinford. As early as the tenth century this road, now the A491, was referred to as Pen Way and was one of the saltways radiating from Droitwich, which traversed the 'Wordsley Brook' valley.

In the late seventeenth century the rural community began to change as coal was being produced in increasing quantities on nearby Pensnett Chase. Local iron was being used in a flourishing nail industry at Wordsley, becoming for a time the main industry of the locality. Coal and the superior local fireclay were major influences leading to the settlement of Lorraine glassmakers in the district in the early seventeenth century. By 1824 there were five glassworks, a cutting shop and a decorating works in Wordsley.

In 1830 Wordsley became a separate ecclesiastical parish. The Kingswinford Glebe Act of 1826 provided for the sale of some glebe land belonging to Kingswinford Rectory, part of the proceeds to build a new rectory, the remainder to be the nucleus of a building fund for a new church in a more central position, more convenient in the extensive developing parish. By 1829 sufficient money was available for the work to start. A site in Wordsley fronting the main road was given by Lord Dudley and Ward, and Lewis Vulliamy (1791–1871), once a pupil of Sir Robert Smirke whose work included the design of the British Museum and the restoration of York Minster, was the chosen architect. The contract was for £6,755: £1,929 from the land sale, £1,600 raised locally and £3,000 from the national £1 million 'Waterloo' fund. The foundation stone was laid by Mr J.H. Hodgetts-Foley, MP of Prestwood Hall on 27 August 1829. The new church, dedicated to the Holy Trinity, was consecrated

Above and opposite: 'A Map of the Parish of Kingswinford in the County of Stafford from a survey made in the year 1822 – Dedicated to the Proprietors of Estates within the said Parish and Published at their request by their obedient servant – William Fowler. Engraved by Neale and Son, 352 Strand.' This interpretation of the Wordsley section was drawn by Eric Richardson in 1999. *(Eric Richardson)*

on 9 December 1837 and became the parish church of Kingswinford. Parish registers and documents were transferred there from St Mary's Church, Kingswinford, which closed, but reopened in 1848 to serve a much smaller area than originally.

In 1888 Staffordshire County Council was established, and in 1894 district divisions of the county were created: Brierley Hill Urban District, Quarry Bank Urban District, and in 1898 Amblecote Urban District. The remainder of the ancient Kingswinford Parish area, including Brockmoor, Pensnett, Wordsley, Kingswinford and Wall Heath, made up the Kingswinford Rural District. Ashwood Hay and Prestwood became part of Seisdon Rural District, now part of South Staffordshire District.

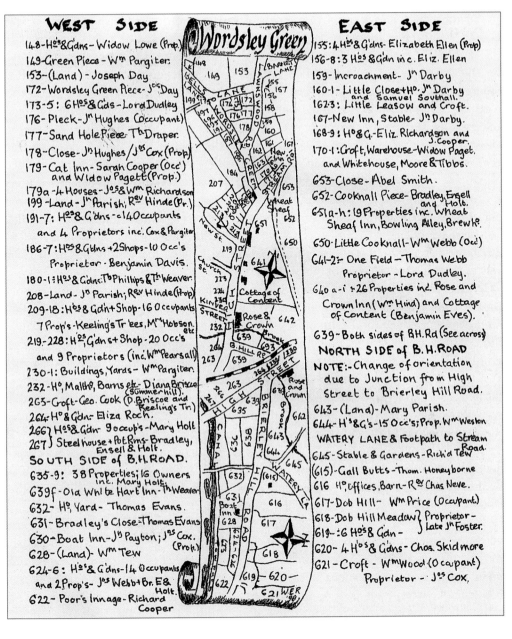

A local government reorganisation in 1934 created a new enlarged Brierley Hill Urban District out of the original Brierley Hill Urban District, which was mainly the area centred around St Michael's Church, Quarry Bank Urban District to the east and Kingswinford Rural District. The proposal that Amblecote Urban District be included was fiercely resisted by its ratepayers, so it was omitted. In 1966 another local government reorganisation took the 1934 Brierley Hill into an extended County Borough of Dudley, yet another in 1974 added to this local authority the Worcestershire Municipal Boroughs of Halesowen and Stourbridge, the latter of which had absorbed Amblecote Urban District in 1966. The resulting huge local authority of some 300,000 people was designated Dudley Metropolitan Borough, and Wordsley is part of it.

William Fowler's 'A Map of the Parish of Kingswinford', 1822, shows only a few buildings on Brettell Lane, the centre of which is clearly marked as 'the boundary with the Hamlet of Amblecote'. Entering Wordsley from the south the first buildings marked on the west side of the main road are the Turk's Head, and on the side of the Stourbridge branch of the Stourbridge Canal, Dial Glass Houses. On the east side of the road are several buildings marked on Audenham Bank, one of which was Audnam Glassworks. Before the hump-backed bridge over the Stourbridge Canal several glassworks are marked. The Park House, known since about 1930 as Wordsley Manor, is shown. The main development went just into Kinver Street, with Kinver Street Glasshouse, and into the present day Brierley Hill Road. The inns marked are the Rose & Crown, the Cottage of Content and the Wheatsheaf on the east side of the main road, and the Cat Inn and the New Inn on the west. The present-day White House near the northern boundary of Wordsley is shown opposite the workhouse. Apart from a few dwellings along present-day Lawnswood Road, the land to the west of the main road was undeveloped at the time of this survey.

By the time of the 1882 Ordnance Survey there had been considerable development. On the 1882 map the north side of Brettell Lane shows considerable development up to Mousebrook Passage, and both sides of Stewkins and John Street were almost full. Brook Street, George Street and Alwen Street were much as they are today. North of Wordsley Brook developments west of the main road were well established: New Street, Wordsley Green, Chapel Street, Queen Street, Rectory Street, and west of the latter, Barnett Lane and Hope Street. Nearly all the gaps shown between houses on the revised OS map of 1901 have now been infilled. The population of Wordsley given in Kingswinford Rural District Council's statistics for 1901 was 5,958.

By 1970 practically every field marked on the nineteenth-century maps had been developed with housing estates, first by local authority housing, and from the 1960s, by private developers. The result is a pleasant suburb just 6 miles from the centre of Dudley and 3 miles from the extensive shopping and commercial complex at Merry Hill. Wordsley is right on the western edge of the West Midlands conurbation adjoining totally unspoilt countryside to the west. All the properties from Hawbush to the junction of Brettell Lane and the main Stourbridge to Kingswinford road are listed as 'houses and gardens'. The footpath marked across plot 303 and as the boundary between plots 298 and 299 still exists today as Mousebrook Passage. The route in this representation continues along Audnam on a different orientation starting at the bottom of Brettell Lane and continuing to the canal bridge. On the south side of the canal are Bradley, Ensell and Holt's glasshouses.

Most of Wordsley village's developments and population were on the west side of the main road and towards Bells Lane. The New Inn (plot 176) and The Cat Inn (plot 175 – Sarah Cooper, occupier, Widow Pagett, proprietress) were two established inns. On the south side of the road junction between High Street and the present Brierley Hill Road (plots 635–9) were thirty-eight properties owned by sixteen people. Plot 643 was occupied by Mary Parish whose descendant sold part of it to the developer of Wordsley Brewery.

1

Holy Trinity Church

Building work commenced in July 1829, the foundation stone was laid on 27 August 1829 and Holy Trinity Church was ready for use in October 1831. On the death of the Revd Nathaniel Hinde, Rector of Kingswinford, in November 1831, the new church became the mother church of the Parish of Kingswinford and the parish records and documents were transferred from St Mary's Kingswinford. The new church was consecrated on 9 December 1831 by Bishop Ryder. At this time the tower was complete with belfry and clock room, but with only one bell and no clock. Five bells were added in 1835–6 by Rudhall of Gloucester at a cost of £236. They were re-hung by Carrs of Smethwick in 1926. The clock was installed in 1835–6 at a cost of £130, the money being raised by voluntary subscription. The original wooden dial clock was replaced in 1926. This view of the church dates from about 1955. (*Author's Collection*)

Wordsley Rectory was built in 1836, financed in part from the sale of some of the glebe lands. After it came into use the original moated Rectory House near St Mary's Church, Kingswinford, was demolished. An exchange of some 14 acres of land near the church and rectory belonging to Thomas William Fletcher of Lawnswood House for some 27 acres of glebe land around his Lawnswood property was granted by the Tithe Commissioners (G. Darby and G.W. Cooke) on 14 August 1863. This 1920s view shows the spaciousness of the rectory, which became too costly to maintain. After demolition in the 1960s the present Rectory Fields houses were built. *(Mike Harris)*

Among the achievements of the Revd George Saxby Penfold DD, Rector, 1832–46, was the establishment of church schools throughout the Parish of Kingswinford. The first was at Kingswinford (1835) and Wordsley's opened in 1842. Additional accommodation was added in 1871, 1873 and 1876. In 1881 there were three departments: boys (287 on roll), girls (232) and infants (186). This early photograph shows the school's position in relation to the church. *(Author's Collection)*

The Revd Charles Girdlestone (1787–1881) was, allegedly, descended from Charlemagne, and certainly related to Nelson. Charles Girdlestone was a member of a prosperous Norfolk family; after a brilliant career at Oxford, he became Vicar of Sedgley in 1826; his was a very active ministry there. After a period in Cheshire he became Rector of Wordsley in 1847. After eight years he went to live in Weston-super-Mare on the grounds of illness, and the eldest of his eight sons, the Revd Henry G. Girdlestone, became curate in charge. Two other sons became curates here, the last one, the Revd A.G. Girdlestone MA, from 1870 to 1887. During his periods of absence the Rector's occasional appearances in Wordsley were noted in the Parochial Church Council's minutes. He was a prolific writer to *The Times* and wrote pamphlets such as 'The South Staffordshire Colliery District – its Evils and their Cures'. *(Author's Collection)*

The Revd John James Slade MA was ordained in 1850 and served for seven years as a curate at St Mary's Church, Kingswinford. He became Vicar of Netherton, and after twenty-one years was nominated by the Earl of Dudley to be Rector of Wordsley, a post he took up in 1878 after which Wordsley finally had a resident Rector. The new Rector increased the number of public services, annual confirmation classes, encouraged support for overseas missions, started the Glynne Mission, opened a mission room in Brook Street, initiated weekly cottage lectures at Brettell Lane, Stewkins and The Green, started a Ragged School, a YMCA and a Church of England Temperance Society. During his incumbency work to beautify the church and make it more able to cope with the increasing range of activities continued, and the Rector played an active role in the campaign to have an art school in the village. He died in 1907. *(Author's Collection)*

The Northwood tomb is situated near the gate at the north-east end of the churchyard. The internationally famous John Northwood I (1836–1902) was the founder of a dynasty of glass men, and the tomb is easily recognised by the stone representation of the Portland Vase. The inscription reads:

In memory of / FREDERICK NORTHWOOD / who died Feb. 13th 1881 / aged 75 years / Also / MARIA NORTHWOOD / his wife who died June 1884 / aged 60 years / Also of their daughters / ELIZABETH who died / August 21 1836 / aged 1 year / MARIA who died / Oct 5 1856 / aged 24 years / MARY ANN who died Oct 13 1856 aged 22 years / In memory of / WILLIAM NORTHWOOD / eldest son of / FREDERICK and MARIA NORTHWOOD / who died April 1 1867 / AGED 39 YEARS / also / SARAH NORTHWOOD / his wife / who died Sep 22 1899 / aged 76 years / also / ELEANOR their daughter / who died March 5 1942 / aged 82 years / In loving memory of / JOSEPH NORTHWOOD / son of FREDERICK NORTHWOOD / who died Nov 15 1915 / aged 76 years / Interred at Bispham Lancs / In memory of / JOHN NORTHWOOD / son of FREDERICK NORTHWOOD / who died at Wall Heath / Feb 13 1902 / aged 65 years / also of ELIZABETH NORTHWOOD / his wife / who died Jan 7 1908 aged 70 years / Also MINNIE NORTHWOOD WHO DIED 1868 aged 31 years / ADA and JOHN / who died in infancy / children of JOHN and ELIZABETH NORTHWOOD / WILLIAM NORTHWOOD / died March 18 1937 aged 79 years.

The tomb was originally white and has a grey stone base.

Stanley Carder, son of Frederick Carder, the famous glass designer, died of kidney failure in 1899, aged seven years. A memorial tomb, designed by Frederick, was erected over the grave in 1901 with end panels depicting an angel, reputedly having a facial resemblance to Stanley. The angel is holding a reversed torch of life and the panels are signed and dated 'F. Carder, 1901'.

Following the theft of four Carder terracotta panels from the then derelict Wordsley Art School in 1993, in a well planned operation over two days, involving scaffolding, ladders, commercial transport and traffic cones outside the old building, attention was drawn to the vulnerability of the Stanley Carder tomb only a few yards away in Wordsley churchyard.

The tomb is in part of the churchyard designated as 'not in use' and maintained by Dudley Metropolitan Borough Council. This maintenance, however, does not include tombs and it was agreed that the Stanley Carder tomb could not be safeguarded in its existing location.

Retired solicitor John Sanders, then Chairman of the Friends of Broadfield House Glass Museum, set about obtaining permission from people and authorities concerned to secure the panels.

In 1998 he went to the USA to visit Gillett Welles Jnr, then in his eighties, son of Frederick's daughter Gladys, who readily gave his approval to the removal plan.

In Wordsley the Revd David Picken of Holy Trinity Church and the Parochial Church Council supported an application to the Consistory Court of the Diocese of Worcester for authority to remove the panels to Broadfield House Glass Museum. After months of negotiation the necessary faculty for the removal of the angel panels was obtained, and in June 2000 Michael O'Neil of Bingham & Sons, Memorial Masons of Wordsley, carried out the required work. Both panels were carefully removed and panels of Balmoral granite were expertly installed in their stead. A casual visitor would not know that the tomb had been altered. *(Author's Collection)*

When researching the life and work of Frederick Carder, the author spent several hours searching Wordsley churchyard for the tomb of Carder's son, Stanley. Eventually it was located on the south side of the pedestrian access to the church, but was covered by brambles and weeds. After an hour's work weed clearing it was possible to take photographs of the tomb. It was in a poor state, with a tilt to one side and weeds growing in the cracks in the cement. However, the panels were intact, and Carder's signature and date clear. *(Author's Collection)*

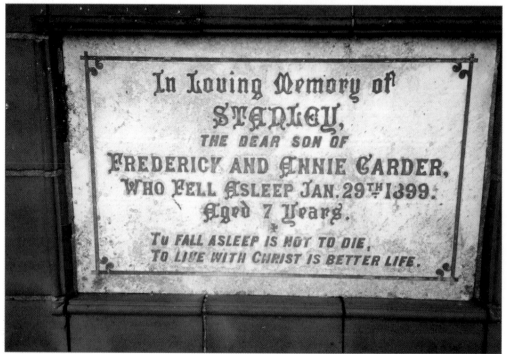

Wordsley War Memorial stands on an island at the entrance of the vehicle access to Holy Trinity Church. Three years after the First World War, on 12 November 1921, the official Unveiling and Dedication Service was held. After prayers and hymns in the church there was a procession to the Cenotaph for an address and unveiling by Major W. Harcourt Webb: 'To the greater glory of God and the memory of the men of Wordsley who gave their lives for King and Country in the Great War, we unveil this monument.' *(Wordsley History Society)*

This was Holy Trinity Church Choir, 1925–6. Back row, left to right: David Banks, Jack Blount, Joe Thompson, Jack Hayward. Middle row: Harry Newman, -?-, Harry Babbs, William Beddard, Jack Titley, -?-. The front row includes Leslie Smart, Walter Griffiths, Billy Hodnet and Frank Perks. *(Wordsley History Society)*

This aerial shot of Wordsley was taken in March 1949 from above Webb's Warehouse, bottom centre. Holy Trinity Church is the dominant building. The bottom left section of the graveyard was reserved for paupers. The two buildings to the left still stand. Except for the Rose & Crown Inn, all the buildings between Church Road access and Brierley Hill Road, including the former School of Art, have been demolished. The old house on the north corner of Kinver Street had connections with Charles II and the battle of Worcester, 1651.

Brierley Hill Road was still built up with Fry's Diecasting recently established next to a former Wordsley Brewery House, near which was the Olympia Cinema and cottages before Watery Lane. Opposite was Wordsley Hall, below that a blacksmith's shop and high above the road Trinity Row. On Kinver Street was Wilf Chance's printing shop, above which the former coach house to The Mount can be seen. After the demolition of the Mount the Mount Road council estate was built in about 1933. Above that is Church Road and to the top left is Belle Vue, jutting into farmland, all of which has been developed since 1960.

Above Church Road is New Street. The Methodist chapel can be seen clearly as can the former Wordsley Post Office building opposite the church entrance. Above the church are Chapel Street and Rectory Street, on the west side of the main road, nineteenth- and twentieth-century housing developments. The white building at the top is Woodfield, which belonged to William George Webb and then to A.E. Marsh, founder of Messrs Marsh & Baxter of Brierley Hill. The house was demolished and houses were built on the site in the 1960s. (Aerofilms)

2

Workhouse & Hospital

(Author's Collection)

In 1776 Stream Piece, the site of Wordsley Hospital, was sold by Thomas Downing to the Earl of Dudley for £173 17s 8d, and in 1784 the original Kingswinford Workhouse was built there.

The Poor Law Amendment Act of 1834 established unions of parishes, which became responsible for a workhouse in each union. The Stourbridge Union covered sixteen parishes from Kingswinford to the Birmingham border, with a total population in 1837 of 36,000. Although there were workhouses in other parts of the union it was decided that the new one under the 1834 Act should be on the Stream Piece site.

The Stourbridge Union spent £3,950 in 1837 on improvements, which included the provision of a borehole and drainage, and in 1838 the Exchequer provided £1,000 for alterations. The altered institution became known as the Stourbridge Union Workhouse.

In 1839 a nailshop was built, and inmates worked on adjoining fields to provide vegetables for their own consumption. The workhouse bakery also provided bread for local grocers. In 1840 1,500 4lb loaves were sold at a profit of £36. In the early twentieth century the workhouse bought railway sleepers and pit props, which were sawn and chopped for firewood and delivered to local shops for resale. This ceased in the 1920s.

Further developments in 1843 included the purchase for £300 of additional land, the Board Room block in 1861, a Girls' Itch Ward and a Boys' Itch Ward in 1883 (for infectious cases). Vagrant sleeping cells were built according to the Local Government Act of 1872.

In 1904 the majority of the buildings were demolished and the replacements became the core of the present hospital.

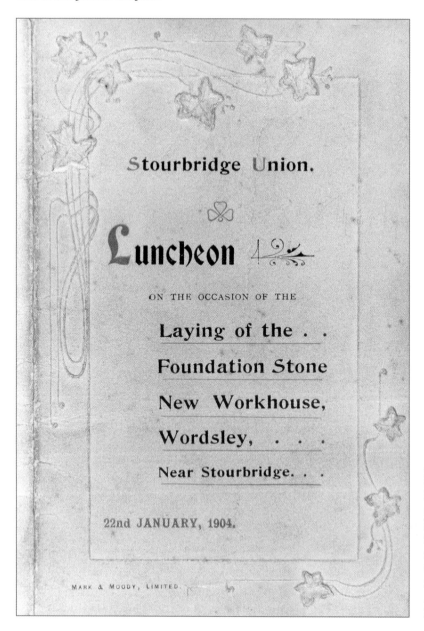

A celebratory luncheon was held on the occasion of the laying of the foundation stone of the new workhouse on 22 January 1904. *(Wordsley History Society)*

The Reception Block. *(Author's Collection)*

The white building in this 1960s photograph was the Second World War Decontamination Building. Left to right: North Ward, D Block, C Block (male imbeciles). *(Author's Collection)*

In early 1915 preparations were made for the workhouse to be turned into a military hospital. The Master was commissioned as a Lieutenant Quartermaster, later as a Captain, for the duration of the First World War. A platoon of the Royal Army Medical Corps under a Sergeant was responsible for stores and equipment. The first intake of wounded soldiers arrived in April 1915, conveyed from Stourbridge railway station by ambulances and trailer ambulances with volunteer drivers. The workhouse became the 1st Southern General Hospital under the command of a Colonel Kirkpatrick. *(Trevor Worton)*

There are almost 100 staff of the 1st Southern General Hospital (Wordsley) in this photograph from the First World War. It includes sixteen men in military uniform, twenty-five women in service uniform and many nurses. The three men in civilian dress were probably local doctors. *(Wordsley History Society)*

Jessie Harris was born on 28 September 1891 at Coalbourne, Amblecote, and in the early 1900s the family of eight children moved to Brook Street. On leaving school Jessie went into service at Enville Hall; during the First World War she worked in a munitions factory. During the war she became a hospital visitor, visiting wounded soldiers who were being treated at Wordsley Hospital. She never married and stayed at home to look after the family. She died on 22 January 1970, following a stroke. *(Mike Harris)*

Alice Mary Harris was born on 11 August 1898 and was disabled from birth, being classified as 'deaf and dumb'. During the First World War she became a hospital visitor with her elder sister Jessie. Despite her handicap she had considerable artistic ability, in which she received guidance from Miss M.H. Richardson, daughter of Mr Benjamin Richardson of Wordsley Hall. Alice's surviving notebooks of her hospital visits include her sketches of patients' regimental badges and autographs of those she was visiting. Her only employment was at her aunt's shop at Brettell Lane. She died on 23 March 1925 aged twenty-six. *(Mike Harris)*

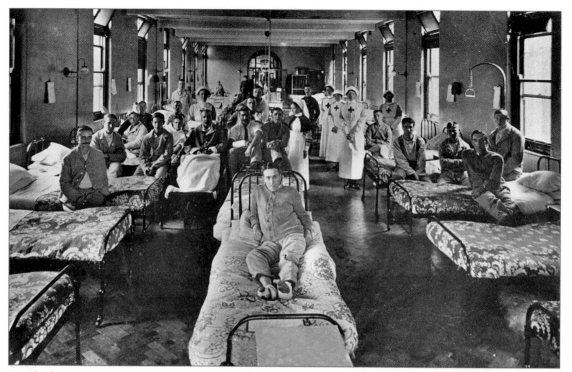

Hundreds of wounded soldiers were cared for at Wordsley Hospital from 1915 to 1920, when the wards were cleared and the military occupation ended. Here recuperating servicemen are shown in a crowded ward. *(Wordsley History Society)*

After the military moved out the infirmary wards were brought back into use, and a maternity ward was opened. Part of the institution was used for the training of a large number of young people with mental disabilities. *(Author's Collection)*

The matron's office, 1940s. The Matron is seen with Sister Cox (on her left) and secretary Doreen Priest (seated). *(Wordsley History Society)*

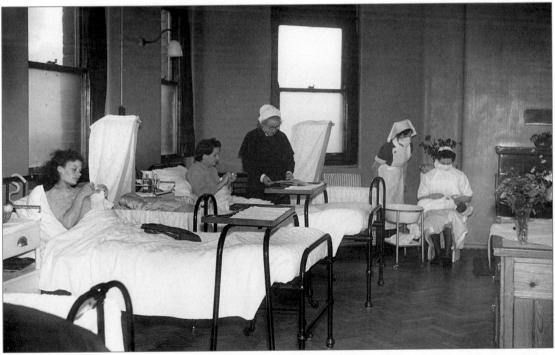

The maternity ward, 1940s. The patient in the first bed on the left is Nellie Thatcher. The staff, left to right: Matron, Nurse, Sister. A new maternity ward was built in the late 1900s. *(Wordsley History Society)*

This view from Pagett's Stream Farm shows the hospital after the early twentieth-century rebuilding programme. Left to right: A and B Blocks, General Stores, E Block, F Block (female), Operating Theatre, O Ward (maternity) C Block, D Block. (*Wordsley History Society*)

The vagrant cells, in the 1960s, were being used for storage, not for their original purpose. *(Author's Collection)*

Opposite: The gardeners at Wordsley Hospital, 1958/9. Standing, left to right: Fred Willetts (Head Gardener), Ken Butters. Seated: Bill Griffin, boy apprentice, Fred Pargeter, Jack Smith, Ron Jones. The building in the background was the piggery where up to forty pigs at a time were reared. Fred Willetts was the pig killer, and at Christmas Prestwood Nursing Home and Wordsley kitchens were supplied with carcasses. Surplus pigs went to Messrs Marsh & Baxter, pig processors of Brierley Hill. The gardeners also produced large quantities of fruit and vegetables. A report of the time praised particularly 'a wonderful collection of apples'. The beautifully kept grounds were a feature of Wordsley Hospital at this period. A new committee in 1960 decided to cease the 'growing for use' aspects of the gardeners' work. *(Wordsley History Society)*

Under the Local Government Act of 1928 the Guardians' duties passed to Staffordshire County Council in 1930, and a local management committee was formed. One of the Guardians' last decisions was to have a clock installed in the hospital tower, which was set to work on 15 April 1930. *(Wordsley History Society)*

In the Second World War the hospital was again used by the military. In 1940 several new wards were built on what had been the sports field. They were first used to accommodate those made homeless in the blitz of 1940/1. As the war progressed, and particularly after D Day, many wounded soldiers arrived. For sometime after 1945 returning British PoWs recuperated in the wards, but after about a year the hospital returned to full civilian use.

Following the 1948 National Health Act the hospital came under the Birmingham Regional Hospital Board. The local administrative body was the Dudley and Stourbridge Group Management Committee, which met at Wordsley, of which Sydney Woodhouse of Quarry Bank was Chairman for many years.

Over the years the hospital has developed to provide medical and surgical wards for men and women, dermatology and general wards, a dental and plastic unit, children's ward, a physiotherapy department, gynaecology, obstetrics and maternity wards, a nurses' home and teaching block, renal unit and kidney machine, pathological laboratory, operating theatre and post-operative care unit, X-ray and outpatients' departments. Support services include a laundry, kitchens, cafeteria, offices and living accommodation.

3

Roads

This late nineteenth-century scene shows the bottom half of Brettell Lane and the tramway, which opened in 1884. The middle of the road became the boundary between Kingswinford Rural District's Wordsley Parish and Amblecote Urban District in 1897. Between 1822 and 1888, according to maps of these dates, most of the land fronting the road had been built upon. A few of those dwellings still remain. *(Author's Collection)*

Some of the original buildings at the bottom of Brettell Lane, early twentieth century. Since then a lot of the buildings at the bottom of the lane have been demolished, left, to make way for road improvements and a supermarket. The buildings beyond Amblecote Furnishers, and on the right, previously in Amblecote Urban District, were knocked down to make way for two huge car showrooms and a municipal care home. (Mike Harris)

The Red Lion Inn in Brettell Lane is one of a block of early properties still left of what was a continuous row of houses from above Mousebrook Passage to the bottom of the road. A full licence was first granted to a James Pagett about 1833. On the left hand side of this remaining block is the late Jim Worton's barber's shop, which he opened in 1930 and was continued by his son Trevor until 2003. (Author's Collection)

Although this 1915 postcard was originally marked 'Lower Brettell Lane', it is actually of the main Stourbridge to Wordsley road at the bottom of the lane. A new Methodist church has replaced the Wesleyan chapel. The two-storey block of properties was demolished in the 1990s and the Crystal Glass Centre built on the site. (H. Jack Haden)

By the beginning of the twentieth century the fronts of the houses on the Wordsley side of the bottom of Brettell Lane had been adapted for use as shops and the lane became a shopping centre for the Amblecote/Audnam community. Left to right: Moody (butcher), W. Hazeldine (grocer), W. Hazeldine (Ladies' & Gentlemen's Hairdressing) with Mr Hazeldine standing in front of his shop (his daughter was the ladies' hairdresser), T.S. Wood (painter and hardware), F.R. Darby (haberdashery). *(Author's Collection)*

This early 1980s view from farther up the lane, looking south, continues the row of shops shown above. Amblecote Furnishers is still trading successfully and a large newsagent's has opened beyond the entry. *(Author's Collection)*

Lidl, the store at the corner of Audnam and Brettell Lane, was designed by Lingfield Securities in 1995 and built by Mowlem Building Contractors. The landscaping was a condition of the local authority's planning consent. In summer the shrubs now screen the interesting glass cone wall feature, which is appropriate for the 'Glass Mile'. The example (visible top left) is one of only four cones left in Britain. Lidl, founded in Germany in the 1930s, became a discount store there in the 1970s with headquarters in Neckarsulm, southern Germany, and is now owned by Dieter Schwarz. The company has 2,300 stores in Germany and 5,600 throughout Europe, of which about 50 are in Britain, and 80,000 employees. In Germany it is about one-third of the size of its competitor Aldi, but Lidl has been more successful abroad. *(Author's Collection)*

Just around the corner, at the bottom of Brettell Lane on the road to Wordsley and opposite the former police station, was G.E. Mountfield's Audnam Garage. In the 1930s the business was also a motor engineer, an agent for Hercules bicycles and a petrol retailer. The latter caused traffic problems in the 1950s, so the owner moved to the present Chemix site on the corner of the main road and Brook Street. The road at this point was eventually improved. *(Ken Rock)*

Next to Lidl on the Wordsley road stands a substantial late Victorian house, Audnam Lodge, which has been a doctor's residence and surgery for well over 100 years. Among the well-known doctors who practised from here were Drs Guy Grindley, Miring, Anderson, Roberts, Tweddell and Yorke Williams. Tastefully restored and redecorated within in 1995, it is part of the Three Villages Practice, the other two being at Wollaston and Kinver. *(Author's Collection)*

The shops at Audnam, just around the corner from Brettell Lane looking towards Wordsley, early 1920s. The ladies standing outside the sweet shop are Alice Harris, in the dark skirt nearest to the shop, Emmy Harris in the print dress, Jessie Harris in white and Mary Harris on the right of the group. Mrs Harris's home-made toffee attracted people from a wide area. The premises of John Guest & Son burnt down in about 1928. It was said that the heat of the fire cracked windows on the opposite side of the road. *(Author's Collection)*

This substantial property was once the local police station. Now it houses a veterinary practice. *(Author's Collection)*

There was a glassmaking works on the site of what is now the Esso Service Station, Audnam, from 1652 until the 1920s. In 1859 William Webb Boulton leased the glassworks from the Earl of Dudley. It became Boulton & Watts when Boulton's cousin, Frederick James Mills, joined him in 1861. The company produced cameo and other specialised decorated glass, and by 1880 had Tiffany & Co. of New York as sole agent in the USA. By 1921 there was a workforce of 120, but their products went out of fashion. Cheap imports and recession led to the closure of the works in 1926, and it was finally demolished in 1928. Recent excavations when renewing petrol tanks enabled Dudley Borough archaeologists to catalogue the extent of the site. *(Author's Collection)*

Harry Harris, wearing a bowler hat, is shown with this impressive car outside the Rose & Crown near Robinson's Nursery on the main road at Audnam. Harry was a foreman glasscutter at the Dennis Glassworks, Amblecote, and lived at Brook Street, Wordsley. (*Mike Harris*)

Robinson's Nursery was between Brook Street and Brettell Lane. Behind the nursery, after 1938, was the sports field of Audnam School, now Brook Primary School. At the south end of this row was the Rose & Crown Inn. This postcard shows the sale notice and the JCB just unloaded prior to demolition, in 1960. Another Rose & Crown Inn survives near the junction with Brierley Hill Road. (*Wordsley History Society*)

Four dozen well-dressed customers, each of whom is wearing a hat, outside the Gladstone Inn at Audnam, early twentieth century. The licensee was Albert Parrish, and a picture of the 'Grand Old Man' is above the door. Originally the inn was part of a terrace of houses, which became a home brew beerhouse and was granted a wine licence in 1888. In 1903 it was rated at £20 per annum, indicative of a fairly large business. *(Wordsley History Society)*

Two substantial buildings in this postcard from about 1910 still stand. The house on the extreme left is The Hollies, a detached, double-fronted house built in about 1905 for a Thomas Price. It has art nouveau windows at the front and back. In the centre is the glass cone that is now the focal point of the Red House Cone Glass Museum. Brook Street Board School was surrounded by a protecting wall, and the first house in unadopted Sutton Street can be seen. The tram carries an advertisement for F.W. Cook's store in Dudley, easily accessible to locals since the introduction of tram lines in 1884. The Hollies was acquired by the Lace Guild in 1984. *(Ken Rock)*

Today The Hollies is the administrative centre of the Lace Guild, with library, exhibition space, committee room and storage. The Lace Guild is an international organisation with a membership of some 6,000, many local groups and a quarterly magazine. When the property was being converted to its present use a number of dog show prize cards were found, together with a photograph of the dog concerned, Amblecote Topper, a rough-haired fox terrier – nine firsts at Bingley Hall, Birmingham, between 1926 and 1933. These cards are now displayed in the hall. *(Author's Collection)*

The opening ceremony of Brook Street Board School was held on 10 November 1884 under the headmastership of Benjamin F. Mason of Wollaston. The Revd George Hodgson was headmaster when the building closed and the school was transferred to the George Street premises of the former Audnam School in 1972. The latter was relocated in new premises in Brierley Hill Road as the Buckpool School. It is now called the Wordsley School. *(Author's Collection)*

This building, known to some as 'The Toblerone' and to others as 'The Wigwams', stands on the site of the former Brook Street Primary School. It is a care home owned and maintained by the Churches' Housing Association of Dudley and District (CHADD). It is administered by Wordsley Housing Society, a registered charity and non-profit-making organisation, managed by a voluntary committee, and registered with the local authority as a residential care home. It provides housing support for people with long-term health problems. Eighteen places are available to people between eighteen and fifty-five years of age who have been referred by Social Services. Residents have their own rooms and optional shared facilities, and staff are on duty twenty-four hours a day. CHADD also manages two smaller houses in Wordsley for residents who are ready to move on. *(Author's Collection)*

Wordsley Royal Knitwear Co., with Webb's Garden Centre (right) and the Red House Glass Cone above it, 1995. The successful company, which had employed up to 120 people, counted Harrow School and Eton College among its customers. In preparation for the opening of the Channel Tunnel it secured a £50,000 order for sweaters for employees of Euro Tunnel. *(A.N. Piddock)*

In 1926 Fred Martin started a small, successful knitwear factory on the Plant Street edge of the grounds trading as Fred Martin Ltd, making 'Royal Wordsley Knitwear'. Ill health forced him to sell the factory, and eventually, in 1939, Horace Piddock, who had a small dress factory in High Street (Winford Manufacturing Co.) and a shop in Market Street, Kingswinford, bought it and transferred the latter to Wordsley. In 1945, the year of Horace Piddock's death, Norman Piddock returned from the forces and took over the factory. In 1948 a second bay and smart frontage were added to the building. A fire in 1951 destroyed what had been Fred Martin's factory, after which the company concentrated on knitwear, with an improved knitting section built in 1959. *(A.N. Piddock)*

The main production room at Royal Wordsley Knitwear Co. with the advanced Swiss- and German-made knitting machines standing on the parquet floor, which attracted thieves' attention when the factory closed in 1995. 120 people had been employed by the company, 100 latterly when Mr Piddock decided to retire, aged seventy-nine. There was no one to succeed him, as members of his family had all pursued their own careers. So Mr Piddock decided to sell the assets – factory and land – and job losses were inevitable. For sixty years this well-known firm had provided work for many local people. *(A.N. Piddock)*

Green Bank House was built on what was plot 636 on Fowler's 1822 Map of Kingswinford. In 1824 the owner was Jonathan Stokes of Fox Farm and the site was occupied by William Webb. A map of 1831 shows a house on High Street, and it seems likely that when this was demolished Green Bank was built sometime between 1831 and 1840 by William Webb or his brother Edward. The Webbs, from then on, were in business as maltsters and corn millers. Here is the front of the house facing north, in the 1990s. From the 1960s it was used as the Royal Wordsley Knitwear Co.'s manager's house. The Red House Glass Cone can be seen above Webb's Garden Centre building. *(Author's Collection)*

The approach to Green Bank Villa (1871 name) was from High Street via a tree-lined carriage drive, which made it quite secluded. In 1881 a solicitor, John Lidstone Holberton, occupied it. Frederick Stuart Jnr, whose father had leased the Red House glass factory in 1881, bought Green Bank in 1901 with approximately 3 acres of land surrounding it. Following this there were several owners of Green Bank. In 1955 Royal Wordsley Knitwear Co. bought the house and grounds from Mr C. Ball. *(Author's Collection)*

By the time the developers were able to start the restoration of the house it was little more than a shell. These photographs clearly show the position of a veranda, which was in place all round the house but was removed in the 1940s. On the lawn at the front there was once an attractive fountain. Wordsley History Society and others campaigned for the house to be saved. *(Author's Collection)*

These recent photographs show how well the developers restored the property, which has a large reception hall, drawing room, dining room and another reception room, fully fitted guest cloakrooms, brand new kitchen, large utility room and large cellarage, including wine cellars. On the first floor there are four en-suite bedrooms and a main house bathroom. There is now a double garage and landscaped garden. On the remaining land from the sale are seventeen attractive detached houses. These and the development on the site of the former Webb's Garden Centre, together with the restored Red House Glass Cone and Museum, present a pleasant approach to Wordsley. *(Author's Collection)*

Norman Piddock, Managing Director (79), with long-serving 75-year-old Miss Doreen Carless, at the 'closing down sale – offers never to be repeated', at the factory on Saturday 25 November 1995. Miss Carless joined Fred Martin Ltd as a finisher in 1934 and later worked for its successor as a winder, machinist and knitter, and for the last fifteen years as store keeper. *(A.N. Piddock)*

This substantial house, built in 1757, plot 261 on Fowler's 1822 map of Kingswinford Parish, once surrounded by parkland, plots 260 and 262, was originally known as The Park House. In the 1830s William Foster lived there and renamed the property Wordsley House. The next occupant was William Robinson Hodgetts of the Red House Glassworks. His daughter, Alice Mary Hodgetts, married Henry Longville Firmstone in 1866, which began the Firmstone connection with the house. Alice's son, George William Hodgetts Firmstone, inherited Wordsley House, which in turn passed to his son, Eldon Lancelot Basil Aubrey Horatio, and daughter, Cecille Rosamund Teresa Hope Bernadine. Eldon, who had renamed the house Wordsley Manor in 1930, died in 1982, and his sister remained there until her death in 1991, when it passed to her nephew, the present owner, Eldon's son, Christopher. He was brought up in Wordsley, attending Bromsgrove School before becoming an architect. He and his wife took up residence in 1991 and set about restoring the house, mainly from his own resources. Wordsley Manor is seen here in its run-down state, and after gradual restoration and improvements over ten years. *(Christopher Firmstone)*

This early seventeenth-century house stood on the north corner of Kinver Street. Here Charles II (as Prince of Wales) called for refreshment after his flight north following defeat at the battle of Worcester in September 1651. He had ridden through Clent, Hagley and Stourbridge before crossing the River Stour into Amblecote. After fording Wordsley Brook Charles ate hurriedly at this house. Many years later he told Samuel Pepys that 'the house afforded no better provision than some small beer, bread and cheese'. The future king travelled to Moseley Hall, Boscobel and Bentley Hall before escaping from Shoreham to France. He was restored to the throne in 1660. The building was demolished in the 1960s before a preservation order could be served. *(Author's Collection)*

The structure adjoining the seventeenth-century house was a twentieth-century addition, which was used by Whitehouses as a butcher's shop. When the whole building was demolished a small shop was erected in its place. *(Wordsley History Society)*

The rear part of the Rose & Crown Inn dates from the late eighteenth century. It has an early nineteenth-century front, which was once part of a terrace of cottages stretching to the corner of Brierley Hill Road, originally Bug Pool Lane, then Brewery Street. The first licensee was James Welling in about 1820. Despite the inn changing hands several times, home brewing continued until 1926. In 1990 Paramount Leisure of Cheshire acquired the premises. It is now the only property left of the original row. Besides what is available inside, the licensee contributes greatly to the area with an attractive annual display of hanging flower baskets. (*Author's Collection*)

Between the Rose & Crown and Brewery Street was a block of five properties, the first of which was Joseph Price's shop. The last was Mr Bayliss's barber's shop. There was an entry in this block leading to small houses in the Rose & Crown yard occupied by Messrs Garrick Thorns and Cheddar Corbett. Between the Art School and the inn was a fish and chip shop owned by Mrs Kinsell and another barber, Mr Halett, whose lather boy, Albert Beasley, went on to play football for Arsenal. Later these properties became Bernard Randle's store. (*Wordsley History Society*)

This postcard view from the bottom of Wordsley High Street was taken before the tramway was laid in 1900. The house with the Charles II connection with a one-storey protrusion is bottom left. A modern shop now stands on the site. The properties on the left up to the bushes are still in use. The white building was Bank House, home of W.H. Stuart until he moved to The Mount on the death of his father Frederick Stuart in 1901. Bank House became the Conservative Club and was renamed Churchill House. When the house was demolished the club transferred to The Mount's coach house, which stood in front of it. The Rose & Crown, licensee W.H. Morgan, is the only building now left at road level between Holy Trinity Church and Brierley Hill Road. *(Wordsley History Society)*

This was the coach house to The Mount, W.H. Stuart's house until he died in 1927. The house was demolished in the 1930s to make way for The Mount estate of council houses. The coach house Conservative Club eventually gave way to a row of nine linked houses. The footpath access to Mount Road was once known as the Bull Run. *(Wordsley History Society)*

The Harmonic Tavern was situated on High Street just below the War Memorial. Once kept by a Mr Workman, it became a private residence before demolition. *(Wordsley History Society)*

This block of shops stands between Church Road and New Street opposite the War Memorial. In 1888, fifteen years after he had established a drapery business in one of these shops, Mr E.C. Witney made his first cassock for Holy Trinity Church. This chance order led to him becoming an internationally known supplier of the highest quality cassocks, surplices, stoles, clerical and academic clothes. By the time of this 1903 photograph the business had expanded to take in the three shops. The premises, which were rebuilt in 1902, with electric light and central heating, then comprised a shop, showroom, office, stockrooms, cutting room and work rooms, and the business rented fifteen additional rooms in Rectory Street. This Wordsley industry employed many women. The premises now house a commission agent and a hairdresser. *(Author's Collection)*

William Henry Collyer came to Wordsley in 1923 from Calverton, Nottinghamshire, after running a successful business there. The frontage of the baker's premises on the corner of New Street and High Street was practically unchanged for sixty years until the business closed in the 1990s and was converted to residential accommodation. In this photograph from about 1930 are, left to right, Harry Smith (a gardener at Beans), Lizzie Collyer, -?-, Jenny Collyer. *(Wordsley History Society)*

This pre-war photograph shows the baker's daughter, Mrs Woodward, née Jenny Collyer, with her daughter Freda and van driver Frank Greenaway. *(Wordsley History Society)*

This substantial property, situated on the main road opposite the Old Cat Inn, belonged to W. Fincher & Son, listed in *Kelly's 1912 Directory of Staffordshire* as painters and decorators. The business later moved to premises at the top of Chapel Street and a dealer in electrical goods, who also charged accumulators for early wireless sets, moved in. Beyond the passage on the right and before the church entrance was Harry Pearson's coalyard. He made local deliveries using a big grey horse. Luke Walters was the last occupant. *(Author's Collection)*

Rectory Farm stood on the main road opposite the New Inn. John Giles, the occupier, delivered milk in the district. The Gileses had three children, Bill, Annie and Elizabeth. *(Wordsley History Society)*

The Cat Inn building dates from the late eighteenth century and was originally two cottages near the corner of Lawnswood Road. An early owner was a Jane Pagett who later bought the corner cottage next to it. Butcher John Cooper appears to have been the first licensee, in about 1810. Margaret Gritton changed the name to the Cat & Cushion in 1851 and Jeremy Bourne changed it back again in 1859. The prefix 'old' was added in 1887. The present owners or their predecessors acquired the inn in 1913 and it was Grade II listed in 1976. Here John Frederick Alwen, licensee 1905–34, stands in front of the pub, early twentieth century. Note the tram timetable under the pub sign. *(Wordsley History Society)*

Mr W. Randall occupied two properties opposite the Cat Inn in Lawnswood Road. The notice above the window of the one on the left states that he was a second-hand furniture dealer, the one above the other window states 'Saddler – all kinds of leather goods made or repaired' and the one over the door that he was licensed to sell tobacco and cigarettes. The door was to the entry at the back of Jack Alwen's fish and chip shop where there was once a stable. *(Wordsley History Society)*

The Drill Hall, given by Col W.G. Webb in the 1880s as HQ for 'D' Coy, the 1st Volunteer Battalion of the South Staffordshire Volunteers. It moved to Brierley Hill in 1905 and the Drill Hall was later purchased by William Haden Richardson of Glasgow, updated and presented to Wordsley in memory of his sister Martha Haden Richardson of Wordsley Hall, who died in 1906. In the 1970s Dudley Borough Council had the hall refurbished and it is now administered by Wordsley Community Association. *(Ken Rock)*

The inscription Richardson Hall can be seen above this 1981 photograph taken from the Old Cat Inn car park. The details on the commemorative plaques beneath the windows are now barely legible. *(Stourbridge News Incorporating County Express)*

Mr Yoxall, a baker, had premises next to Richardson Hall. He used a horse and cart to make deliveries. The access to the horse's stable behind the shop was via an entry. *(Wordsley History Society)*

The Old Red Lion stood on the corner of The Green and Lawnswood Road. When this area was redeveloped in the second half of the twentieth century a new inn with a car park was built well back from the road. *(Wordsley History Society)*

These cottages on Wordsley Green, at the back of which was New Street, were marked on the 1881 Ordnance Survey map. There was an access to the right of the street lamp leading to a terrace of five properties known as The Back Houses. Among those who lived there were the Carters, Mallens, Parsons and Poultons, who sold coal. All of the old cottages were demolished during the second half of the twentieth century. *(Wordsley History Society)*

Ivy House Cottage on The Green was occupied by a Miss Cooper. The next occupant was her nephew, Bill Downes, who was once a glass blower in London but is remembered locally as the owner of an early wireless set, as a window cleaner and crossword puzzle prizewinner. The house burnt down in the late 1960s, after which the site was cleared. Its position can be pinpointed, as the horse chestnut tree which was in the garden still stands. *(Wordsley History Society)*

These properties were situated near the junction of what was The Green and what is now Bells Lane. The bay window was part of the Royal Exchange Inn, actually on Wordsley Green. The Raven Inn was just around the corner. These two inns and the George & Dragon Inn were all on the 1881 OS map, all brewing their own beer. *(Wordsley History Society)*

Both the George & Dragon and the Raven stood on what is now Bells Lane. Harry Partridge of New Street is the customer who paused to have his photograph taken before being served. *(Wordsley History Society)*

Woodfield House, an early to mid-nineteenth-century substantial construction that lay between Lawnswood Road, then Prestwood Road, and Cot Lane, on plots 2005–10 on Fowler's 1822 map of the Parish of Kingswinford. It was once the home of Colonel William George Webb, whose family wealth came from glass, seeds, hops and so on, later of William Harcourt Webb and then of Alfred Edward Marsh, son of the founder of Messrs Marsh & Baxter Ltd, pig processors of Brierley Hill. (*Wordsley History Society*)

The size of the gardening staff at Woodfield gives an indication of the extent of the land surrounding the house. The back row includes Horace Smith, Chris Richardson, Jack Haywood, Frank Green (Head Gardener). Seated: Frank Lawton, -?-. After the demolition of the house in the 1960s an attractive housing estate was erected on the site by Messrs Fletcher. (*Wordsley History Society*)

Brewery Street dressed for the carnival, shown from near the main road, 1930. The little girl is Jean Whitehouse, aged three. In the doorway below the shop are Mrs King and daughter Nellie and above the shop are Mr and Mrs Fletcher. Properties above included the Bear Inn, a Mr Richardson's house, Stuart's glass cutting shop, Wordsley Brewery and the Lion Hotel, on which site the Olympia Cinema was built in 1912. Beyond Watery Lane was Field House. After the Second World War Fry's Diecasting Works occupied the site where these properties once stood. When Fry's pulled out in the 1990s the site was cleared and thirty-one houses were built on it. *(Malcolm Penn)*

This view from the Greenbank area shows where the John Parrish glassworks stood on the north side of Brewery Street, *c.* 1930. (On Fowler's 1822 map, plot 643, it is shown as having been occupied by a Mary Parrish.) It was bought by Stuarts in 1910, but closed temporarily in 1931 because of the recession. The glasshouse closed in 1934, but the cutting shop continued operating until 1942. The chimney-stack was demolished in 1946 and the site used by Fry's Diecasting Works. *(Wordsley History Society)*

In 1912 Anthony Bayley converted a part of Wordsley Brewery into a cinema that could hold 600 people. He ran it for the next decade, and such was its popularity that he felt it necessary to employ a policeman at 8s a night to control the crowds. However, ill health forced Bayley to sell the business to Cecil Couper in 1923. In 1934 it was taken over by Fred Leatham and Eldon Firmstone of Wordsley Manor. In 1940 the cinema was bought by Mr Bullock who employed Mick Masters on security. The last film, *Maracaibo*, starring Cornel Wilde, was shown on 16 May 1959. *(Author's Collection)*

The Olympia Cinema was acquired by neighbouring Fry's Diecasting in 1959 and remained unused for ten years. It was demolished in 1969 when a foundation stone for the original brewery, dated 1858, was found. The aperture through which the films were projected can be seen on the left. *(Stourbridge News Incorporating County Express)*

The White House on the corner of Mill Street and Brewery Street was the home of Owen Gibbons in the 1880s. Before demolition the house was occupied by Dr Tweddell. On the right are cottages which stood above Watery Lane and just past the bend in the road, beyond cottages that were below the lane, is the Olympia Cinema. *(Author's Collection)*

Field House stood in Brewery Street just above Watery Lane and in the early nineteenth century was the home of the Ensell (glassmakers) family. In the early twentieth century it became the home of Arthur Richardson, and in the 1950s was occupied by a builder. The house was demolished in about 1990. *(Author's Collection)*

This 1940s view taken from the drive of the White House shows the upper part of Brierley Hill Road. Today, halfway up the road on the left is the access to a late 1940s housing development, Swiss Drive. At the top of the road the cutting through the sandstone, an attraction to geology students, is much as it was in the 1850s when the road to Brierley Hill was improved under a parish-inspired initiative to occupy some of the unemployed. *(Wordsley History Society)*

The Old Boat Inn on the upper part of Brewery Street, roughly opposite the Swiss Drive access today, was another home brew establishment. In 1900 the licensee was Daniel Gill. *(Wordsley History Society)*

Wordsley Hall is a late eighteenth-century Grade II listed two-storey building just inside Mill Street from Brierley Hill Road and near to The White House. The wing on the right was a late nineteenth-century addition. In 1851, with two sons, four daughters and a servant, Benjamin Richardson, a leading Wordsley glassmaker, lived there. He died in 1887, but his daughter, Martha Haden Richardson, continued to live there until her sudden death in 1906. This fine building is now Wordsley Hall Rest Home. (*Author's Collection*)

The Samson & Lion Inn dates from the opening of the Stourbridge Canal in 1779. The dock at the rear became important for local industry and the inn served bargees and their horses for which stables were built. As at many early inns beer was home brewed. Coalmaster Thomas Baker was the first recorded landlord in 1820. In 1880 Samuel Hill became the tenant and in 1893 bought the property for £400. Part of the premises was later used for furniture sales. It was sold to Ansell's Brewery of Aston in 1940. In the late twentieth century it became part of the Marston, Thompson, Evershed Group. Under its present management it is an attractive traditional canal hostelry with several bedrooms for guests, and outside there is an eye-catching floral display to greet visitors entering Wordsley from The Leys. (*Author's Collection*)

John Collett was appointed headmaster of the National School in 1877. He married Fanny Holmes of Junction House and they settled at 1 New Street. Here they are seen with two of their four children sometime in the late nineteenth century. *(Wordsley History Society)*

Foundation stones were laid for the new Primitive Methodist Church in New Street on 19 June 1882 by Mrs G. Bourne, Mrs W. Davies, Mrs C. Blackshaw and the Revd C. Dudley. Originally there were two main rooms and basic facilities included earth closets, coke stoves, gas lighting and a harmonium. A thriving church developed. In 1901 there were 158 scholars on the roll and 20 Sunday School teachers. Services and social activities were well attended. Minor building improvements were ongoing and in 1953 there was an extended programme of improvements. Sadly, in recent years church membership has declined, and as the building does not meet modern requirements it seems likely to close soon and the congregation will join neighbouring churches. *(Author's Collection)*

The Bird in Hand Inn stands on the corner of John Street and Bridge Street. The name originally had associations with the sport of hawking. Elijah Collins had a grocery shop in part of the building, converted part of it to a beerhouse and bought beer in. The property had three owners before being acquired with other inns belonging to H. Newman & Son Ltd by Wolverhampton & Dudley Breweries in 1960. Outwardly the inn is little changed from Elijah Collins's day. *(Author's Collection)*

The 1901 OS map (71.06) shows John Street fully built up, whereas on Fowler's 1822 map this area had no buildings. The typical mid- to late nineteenth-century cottages all look well kept and the one-way north to south traffic order has greatly improved this completely residential road. *(Author's Collection)*

One of the oldest houses in Wordsley, Rose Cottage, just inside Barnett Lane from Lawnswood Road, is clearly marked on Fowler's 1822 map (plot 156). It was once an inn named The Sign of the Finger. For many years it was occupied by the Ryder family. The last occupant, a Miss Ryder, kept a collection of animals in the extensive paddock behind the house. After her death the property was sold, the cottage beautifully restored and houses built behind it. *(Author's Collection)*

4

Industry

A painting of William Haden Richardson (1785–1876) from Broadfield House Glass Museum. He was the eldest of the eleven children of Joseph Richardson. In 1810 William joined Dudley Flint Glass Works, where his father had built the glass cone, and he became the firm's traveller. With younger brothers Benjamin and Jonathan, as W.H.R. and J. Richardson, he became part of a leading, world-famous glass manufactory. For many years he lived in London and acted as the firm's representative there. (*Broadfield House Glass Museum*)

Benjamin Richardson (1802–87) was the ninth child of Joseph Richardson, a master glasshouse furnace builder, of Wordsley. From his position at Thomas Hawkes's glassworks in Dudley, Benjamin was appointed by the Wainwright brothers, owners of Wordsley Flint Glass Works, as their manager. After a year Benjamin was joined by his brother William and Thomas Webb to form the firm Webb & Richardson. They had a five-year lease from the Wainwrights, which was renewed in 1834. Thomas Webb withdrew from the company in 1836 and the Richardson brothers were joined by their younger brother, Jonathan. In 1842 the firm became W.H., B. and J. Richardson. (*Broadfield House Glass Museum*)

The Glass Makers' Certificate, probably designed by Benjamin Richardson, is thought to date from September 1849 when the society was reorganised on the lines of the 'New Model' unions. The central large illustration is of the interior of a glasshouse, on its left the exterior and on the right the interior of a showroom. The top figure is the Goddess of Fame crowning the designer on her right and the workman on her left with laurel leaves, representing the alliance of Art and Manufacture. The next figures, below, represent Justice (left) and Truth (right), and the figures on either side are illustrations from Aesop's Fable of the Bundle of Sticks. The certificate is 22.5in by 19.6in wide. (*Charles Hadjamach*)

Henry Gething Richardson (1832–1916) was described in 1861 as a flint glass manufacturer, and in 1871 when he lived in Collis Street he employed eighteen people. He later moved to Hawthorn Cottage next to Wordsley Hall. He took over the family business in about 1881. *(Broadfield House Glass Museum)*

John Northwood (1836–1902) was the second son born to parents who kept a small general shop at the bottom of Wordsley High Street. At the age of twelve he went to work at W.H., B. & J. Richardson's Wordsley Flint Glass Works where he received training in glass decoration. In 1859 John, with his younger brother Joseph, H.G. Richardson and Thomas Webb, opened a glass decorating workshop at the junction of Lawnswood Road and Barnett Lane. After a year Richardson and Webb left and the firm traded as J. & J. Northwood. Here John Northwood created some of the world's most famous pieces of glass, such as the Portland Vase replica, the Milton Vase and the Pegasus Vase. In 1882 John became works manager and artistic director of Stevens & Williams, Brierley Hill. The Wordsley enterprise continued until 1927 when it was sold and demolished. *(Broadfield House Glass Museum)*

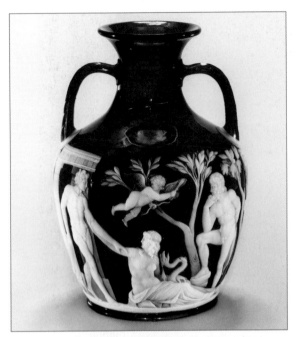

The Portland Vase is a masterpiece of ancient Roman cameo glass. In 1784 it came into the possession of the Duchess of Portland, after whom it is named. It was deposited in the British Museum in 1810 and remained there on loan until 1945, when the museum finally bought it.

John Northwood, when working for the Richardsons, had heard Benjamin Richardson say that he would give £1,000 to any craftsman who could reproduce the famous Portland Vase in glass. This was always in his mind.

In the 1870s Northwood's cousin, Philip Pargeter, was manufacturing glass at the Red House Glass Works. One of his glassmakers, Daniel Hancock, managed to make an accurate blank of the vase. Northwood spent three years carving it with tools he designed, and he travelled several times to the British Museum to compare his progress with the original. It was completed in 1876 and exhibited locally.
(Broadfield House Glass Museum)

Frederick Carder was a schoolboy protégé of John Northwood I, at the latter's works in Wordsley. He joined Stevens and Williams as an apprentice glass designer in 1880. He emigrated to the USA in 1903 where he established the famous Steuben Glass Works, which was absorbed by Corning Glass Works in 1917. He continued to work for Steuben until he was 96. He died on 11 December 1963, aged 100.
(Broadfield House Glass Museum)

The Northwood family, late nineteenth century. Back row, left to right: Charles Attwood, Clarence Northwood (son of Clara Elizabeth and Harry), Jack Bradley, Dave Campbell. Third row: Louise Northwood and husband Fred, Carl Northwood and wife Rose, Winifred Northwood Meredith, May Northwood Bradley, John Northwood I, Will Meredith, Lennie Guy (later married Ethel Northwood). Second row: Ina Northwood Attwood, Clara Elizabeth Beaumont Northwood, Elizabeth Duggan Northwood, Eva Northwood Campbell, Ethel Northwood, Harry Northwood. Front row: Elsie and Alice Northwood (daughters of Louise and Fred), Mabel Virginia Northwood (daughter of Clara Elizabeth and Harry), Marie Northwood (daughter of Fred and Louise). *(Broadfield House Glass Museum)*

The Glasscutters Arms in Barnett Street is the only visible reminder of J. & J. Northwood's small 'factory in the country', which was established in 1860 and continued until 1927 when the site was sold and later developed. As the majority of the employees were women, it seems unlikely that they would have been regular customers at the pub. William Newman was the first landlord in 1868 of what was a single-room beer house, big enough to cater for the few houses in this new street off Barnett Lane; there were only four houses on the 1871 Census and seven on that of 1891. The inn remained in the Newman family until 1926. Since then there have been several owners, the latest being Nomura. It is now a well-kept local with a thriving bowls club using its excellent green. *(Author's Collection)*

This painting by Henry L. Pratt, *c.* 1846, shows industrial Wordsley. The Red House Glass Cone is in the middle of the painting, the left of the three prominent cones. The middle one is that of the White House Glassworks on the opposite side of the main Stourbridge to Kingswinford road, built between 1779 and 1785. The third cone is that of Messrs W.H.B. and J. Richardson built in 1842. The substantial house on the extreme right is Wordsley House, originally Park House; it was renamed Wordsley Manor in 1930. (*Broadfield House Glass Museum*)

Henry Gething Richardson, second son of Benjamin Richardson, worked as a glass decorator for twenty years before taking over the family business in about 1881. This advertisement in the *Pottery Gazette* of 1 July 1899 shows the extent of the Wordsley Flint Glassworks, perhaps with some artistic licence. The building at the side of the canal has long since gone, but some of the other buildings are still used as business premises. (*Broadfield House Glass Museum*)

This painting, *c.* 1840, shows the furnace inside the Richardson glass cone at what was then the Wordsley Glassworks. The glassworkers are shown carrying out their tasks around it, at the furnace, blowing and shaping. This was a familiar scene until as late as 1936 at the Red House Glass Cone, and in the nineteenth and early twentieth century at many local glass factories. *(Broadfield House Glass Museum)*

In 1859 Henry G. Richardson, T. Guest, John Northwood I and his brother Joseph set up a small glass decorating business near the junction of Lawnswood Road and Barnett Lane. They erected buildings comprising cutting rooms, an acidising shop and warehouse, and there was a steam boiler and stack. The partnership was dissolved after about a year but the business continued as J. & J. Northwood. With John, the inventor and innovator of machines, to improve decorating processes and Joseph, the administrator, the firm became very profitable.

This 1885 photograph of part of the decorating shop shows a geometrical etching machine with a female operative. On the left is James Hill, a former outstanding student of Stourbridge College of Art. *(Author's Collection)*

Richard Bradley purchased the Red House site in 1788. The cone was probably built between 1788 and 1796. After the site had been operated by lessees or owners up to 1852 it was taken over by Edward Webb, and in 1869 it was leased to Philip Pargeter. He left in 1881 when the lease was taken over by Frederick Stuart (1816–1900), thus beginning a 114-year family involvement. The firm purchased the site in the 1920s. In 1995 Stuart Crystal was bought by Waterford Crystal plc and closed in November 2001.

This photograph appeared in 1902 in an article about the Red House Glassworks in the *Gentleman's Magazine*. The cone is 90ft high and 60ft in diameter. It houses a furnace in the middle, around which the glassmakers worked. It acted as a giant chimney, the glass furnaces drawing air through underground tunnels to increase the temperature to a high-enough point to melt the ingredients. This example was used by Messrs Stuart Crystal until 1936 and then used for storage. In 1966 it was designated a Grade II listed building.

In 2001 Dudley Metropolitan Borough Council started a comprehensive renovation of the site with a grant of £350,000 from Advantage West Midlands, £375,000 from the Heritage Lottery Fund, £570,000 from the European Development Fund, £119,000 from English Heritage and £11,500 from Messrs Stuart Crystal. (*Broadfield House Glass Museum*)

The glass furnace stood in the centre of the cone. It was circular in shape, about 23ft in diameter, 10ft high and held between ten and twelve melting pots, which stood in a ring in the furnace with their mouths opening outward and within the cone. The pots were made of special refractory fireclay, capable of withstanding the high temperature (1,400°C) in the furnace. The glass blower, shown here in 1902, has gathered the metal (molten glass) from the pot on his hollow blowpipe and is shaping the piece. *(Broadfield House Glass Museum)*

This craftsman, watched by his workmates, is trimming the glass. The tools of the trade have hardly changed in design over several centuries. Note the robust, simple glasshouse 'furniture'. *(Broadfield House Glass Museum)*

The newly made articles are placed in an annealing oven or lehr, a long, low, arched chamber, heated at the end that opens into the glasshouse. Then they were loaded on to an iron tray in the hottest part of the oven and pulled to the other end, which was at about room temperature. When cooled gradually articles are less likely to break. Here a boy is placing an article in the lehr. *(Broadfield House Glass Museum)*

During the evolution of most crafts, machines have been developed to speed up processes, and the glass-making crafts were no exception. Here these glassmakers are in the cone operating a threading machine. The machine was used for winding a spiral trail around the glass. *(Broadfield House Glass Museum)*

A Stuart cutting shop, 1902. The steam-driven shaft ran the length of the roof and had pulleys with continuous leather-belt connections with the decorators' individual machines. All the operatives in this workshop at that time were men. *(Broadfield House Glass Museum)*

The Stuart directors, *c.* 1927. Back row, left to right: F.C. Pauli, W.E. Cook (Stuart), F.C. Stuart, G.W. Stuart. Front row: E.M. Stuart, F.H. Stuart, R. Stuart, S.M. Stuart, W.A. Stuart. *(Ian M. Stuart)*

Stuart workers in front of a 1916 structure which was built between the White House Cone and the canal, early 1920s. Ted Hands is third from the right on the back row, and Isaiah Price, with pipe, who lived in Belle Vue, is in the centre of the middle row. *(Broadfield House Glass Museum)*

Stuart workers, early 1930s. Back row, left to right: 2nd Jim Clark, 4th I. Richards. Front row: 2nd Arthur Bishop, 4th Jack Druce. *(Broadfield House Glass Museum)*

The Stuart Athletic Club cricket team won the Corbett Hospital Cup Competition in 1937. Back row, left to right: W. Weeton, Sid Perks, W. Mason, L. Lee, S. Smith, B. Kinnear, G. Drake. Middle row: includes J. Rowbottom, S. Gill and H.E. Davies (Captain). Front row: L. Lewis, L. Zinke. *(Wordsley History Society)*

Stuart & Sons staff Christmas party, 1960. *(Wordsley History Society)*

The opening of the Stourbridge Canal in 1779 led to the building, in 1778, of a new glassworks on the Audnam side of the waterway at the bottom of Stewkins. With two cones, one for bottle glass, the other for broad glass, a prosperous business trading as John Piddock & Sons developed. Fowler's 1822 map of Kingswinford (plot 291) shows the buildings labelled as 'Dial Glass Houses'.

As with many businesses of the period, the Dial Glassworks changed hands many times until a Mr and Mrs Plowden and a Mr Thompson started Plowden & Thompson in 1922. In about 1924 Richard Threlfall joined the firm, which still has a family connection. During the Second World War the firm's speciality of hand-drawn precision tubing and rods was in great demand for the war effort. Postwar research into production techniques ensured the company's future. In March 2000 Plowden & Thompson Ltd bought the rights to use the 'Tudor Crystal' brand, so their crystal glass is now being produced in the old Dial cone. With a staff of about fifty the firm is the last of such size in the Stourbridge district. (*Tudor Crystal*)

Stourbridge Glass Co. Ltd was established in 1921 at the end of Junction Road, Wordsley, and on the side of the Stourbridge Branch Canal. Starting with about 70 employees, about half of whom were experienced craftsmen from other large local firms, the workforce increased to about 250 at its peak. The firm officially changed its name to Tudor Crystal (Stourbridge) Ltd in 1972. Production of high-quality goods continued until April 1994 when the last 10 workmen were made redundant. This photograph shows the entrance to the works from Junction Road. (*Wordsley History Society*)

Stourbridge Glass Co. employees assembled outside the works in the interwar period (above) and sometime after 1945 (below), standing on Chubb's Bridge over the Stourbridge Branch Canal. *(Broadfield House Glass Museum)*

A view of Stourbridge Glass Co. from the Stourbridge Branch Canal. (*Broadfield House Glass Museum*)

William Webb and Sons, founded in 1861, had huge premises at Wordsley. The 1889 catalogue mentions 'another large warehouse 120 feet by 50 feet, 75 feet high with 6 floors for the careful execution of orders for vegetable seeds, flower seeds and bulbs'. This 1940s aerial view shows the extent of the Webb buildings (centre). To the right of the buildings, bordering Brewery Street, were ten greenhouses between which and the canal were seed growing areas. Dadford's Warehouse is shown bottom left. The main buildings were demolished in the 1970s and the hop warehouse in 1990. (*Wordsley History Society*)

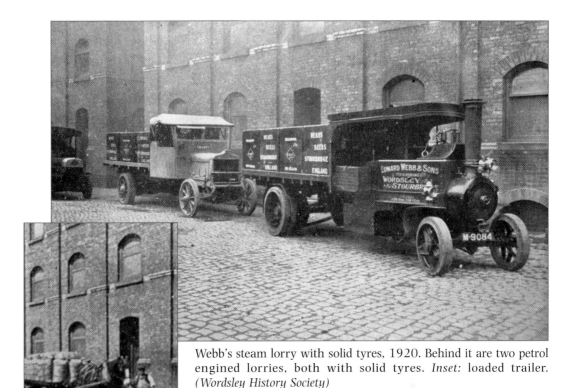

Webb's steam lorry with solid tyres, 1920. Behind it are two petrol engined lorries, both with solid tyres. *Inset:* loaded trailer. *(Wordsley History Society)*

This late nineteenth-century advertising postcard, in which the designer may have exercised some artistic licence, not uncommon at the time, proudly advertises Webb's most prestigious customers and the title 'Royal Seed Establishment'. Other important customers included the head gardeners at Chatsworth, Longleat and Ingestre Hall, and the Rt Hon. Joseph Chamberlain MP. *(Wordsley History Society)*

Webbs
R.H.S. Vegeta
which obtained THE ONLY GOLD MEDAL awar
The Garden.—" A magnificent collection of exceptic

Webb's exhibited regularly and their successes were depicted on postcards such as this late nineteenth-century one. Names they gave to seeds made local places known throughout the world, e.g: Wordsley Wonder (pea) and Stourbridge Glory (seed potato). (*Wordsley History Society*)

Webb's catalogues were more than just price lists for seeds and gardening tools. They were mini-gardening books with detailed instructions for successful gardening. The company was a great supporter of gardeners' clubs and societies and made much of its special prizes of cash or seeds offered for competition at horticultural shows at all levels. The 1889 catalogue lists over 100 societies from Abingdon to the Yorkshire Gala to which show prizes were given. These were accompanied by certificates such as the one illustrated here. (*Wordsley History Society*)

The hop warehouse was all that remained of the large Webb complex to the east of Mill Street. After a while the site was redeveloped for houses. The last reminder locally of this famous firm was a small garden centre on the main road and side of the canal, which also finally gave way to housing development. (*Geoff Warburton*)

5

The Stourbridge Canal

The cottages at The Dock, off Brierley Hill Road, were built after the Stourbridge Canal linking the Birmingham system with the Staffordshire and Worcestershire Canal at Stourton was constructed in 1779. They are shown on Fowler's 1822 map. Originally there were six cottages, a smithy and stabling. The buildings are now combined into one establishment, a residence, general stores and off-licence, which serves present-day users of the canal as well as people living nearby. The locks in descending order are nos 9, 10 and in the foreground 11. *(Author's Collection)*

The lock cottage is in excellent condition. To the south and behind it is a large pound, which is connected to the pound between locks 9 and 10 by a large culvert. From the pound between locks 8 and 9 there is an overflow to the tail of lock 10. The old outside toilet of the lock cottage was situated over this overflow channel, a usual practice at nineteenth-century lock cottages. *(Author's Collection)*

The cantilever bridge at the foot of lock 9, dating from 1827, is of 'split' design. This was to enable the towrope of boats to slip through to facilitate the working of horse-drawn boats. The split bridge has a cast-iron deck and wrought-iron handrails. *(Author's Collection)*

Looking west from lock 10, this view shows a leisure boat approaching a prepared lock 11. The roving bridge on the left gave access to a pound which provided mooring, possibly for boats awaiting their turn in a dry dock, formerly on the opposite side of the canal, which was filled in about 1910. The 1796 Red House Glass Cone is the dominant feature which stands near the Glasshouse Bridge on the main road. The opening of the canal in 1779 gave great impetus to the local glass industry and a number of glass manufacturers were shareholders. The canal enabled a great advance to be made in the transport of raw materials and finished products. *(Geoff Warburton)*

The wooden trans-shipment warehouse by lock 12, known as Shed Lock, built by the canal company towards the end of the nineteenth century, was used by Ivy Mills, later Webb's Seeds, and also for hops by nearby Wordsley Brewery. One side was open to the canal and the roof was supported by iron columns. It is said that the original building was burnt down and the warehouse rebuilt. The columns away from the canal have rainwater outlets, which now have no use but may have had on the original structure. At one time the warehouse was operated by Thomas Bantock, a carrier for the Great Western Railway, and it was known as the Railway Shed, although the nearest railway siding was at Brettell Lane. There was also a coal wharf adjoining the site supplied by canal. *(Stourbridge News Incorporating County Express)*

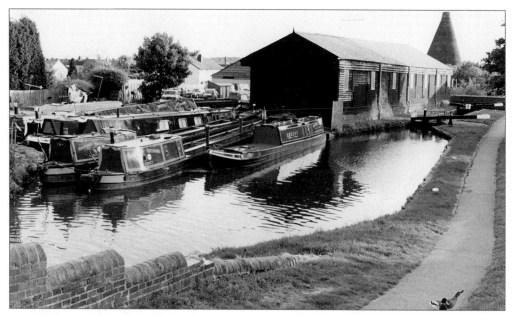

The site now named Dadford's Wharf after Thomas Dadford Jnr, the canal engineer, is now a hive of activity. It was in a derelict state when leased from British Waterways in 1995 by Messrs I.F. Kemp Restoration Services, whose first task was to restore the building. Ian Kemp restores riveted boats – he worked on the Black Country Living Museum's steam narrowboat *President*. He shares the site with Dave Harris, a boat builder, and Philip Speight, a boat painter. In this view Dadford's Bridge is top right. *(Author's Collection)*

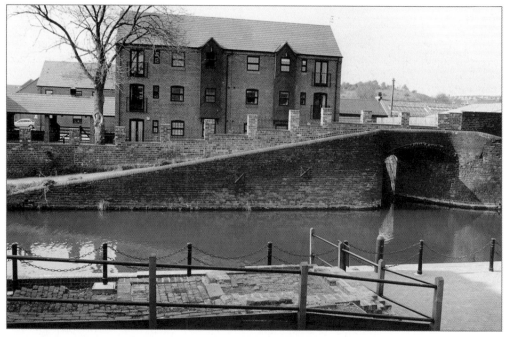

This view taken from the Red House Glass Cone canal access shows the roving bridge that spans what was the entrance to Joburn's Basin, 2003. In its day this served the adjacent iron and brass foundry. The area was recently used by Webb's Garden Centre. The recent housing development on that site and the redevelopment of the Red House Glass Cone site have become two attractive canalside features. *(Author's Collection)*

The canal manager's house slightly to the east of the junction with the Stourbridge Branch with a steam pleasure boat and a rowing boat in the foreground, *c.* 1900. A later view shows an additional structure on the west side. There are no buildings on the site now. *(Author's Collection)*

This postcard view through the roving bridge of the Stourbridge Arm of the canal shows the bottom lock of the Stourbridge 16 (no. 16). A large house, possibly the canal manager's, was situated on the left of the canal and opposite were a cottage and toll office. In the 1940s Shillingfords hired out rowing boats from the house on the right. *(Author's Collection)*

Joseph Hammond, a barber of 3 Camp Hill, adorned the walls of his shop with his paintings. This one, from about 1925, is of Junction House at the junction of the Stourbridge Canal and the Stourbridge Arm. His solicitor, A.G. Rudge, liked the painting and was given it by the family after Joseph's death. It is now on display in Wordsley. *(David Eades)*

In 1917 it was reported that Messrs A.H. Guest, local building contractors, were experimenting in the use of concrete in boat building. This arose because of the shortage of normal materials during the First World War. The experimental boat was built largely by female labour, had a draught of less than 2ft and was supposed to carry 25 to 30 tons of cargo. Sceptics expressed similar doubts to those raised when 'Iron Mad' Wilkinson launched his iron canal boat in 1787. However, the concrete boat floated, as can be seen in this 1918 photograph of the Stourbridge Branch near Guest's builder's yard. (*Wordsley History Society*)

In practice, the concrete boat project foundered. Estimate of draught and load capacity proved to be inaccurate. Because of its weight, only a light load could be carried and this was uneconomic. Two such boats were made and they eventually found their way to the pound below lock 13 on the Stourbridge Canal near Stuart Crystal, where they were used for bank protection on the opposite side to the towpath. In the winter of 1988/9 one, seen here, was carefully removed from the bank and taken to the National Waterways Museum, Gloucester. (*Wordsley History Society*)

6

Schools

This building was a Congregational chapel originally, built as an offshoot of
Stourbridge Congregational church in about 1830, and when abandoned as a place of
worship it was used as Wordsley Institute. In the early 1890s Wordsley Art School
classes moved from Brook Street School to the old chapel. This photograph, on which
'Wordsley Art Class' can be seen above the door, was taken just before its demolition
in 2000. *(Broadfield House Glass Museum)*

A Wordsley evening art class had been established in the 1860s, and may have been held at the Wordsley Mechanics' Institute on the High Street. On 1 September 1885 Kingswinford School Board gave permission for a night school to be held at Brook Street Board Schools, and the first evening art class was held on 28 September 1885. A week later a science class was established.

Owen Gibbons, who had come to live in Wordsley, took the evening art class, and Mr B.F. Mason, head of the day school, took the science class. Soon there was a large attendance at both classes, which was maintained. From the outset art classes were related to the local industries of glass and pottery, and were conducted under the auspices of the City & Guilds of London Institute. There were early successes in the external examinations, the school's first silver medal in 1888, gold and bronze medals in 1889 and another silver in 1890.

In the early 1890s the Kingswinford School Board terminated the agreement for staging the evening classes in art and science, though, strangely, it agreed to the establishment of evening classes in cookery, gardening and wood turning. Mr Gibbons, the head, with the agreement of his committee, obtained the use of Wordsley Institute for his part-time students. The advanced students he arranged to teach in his own home, where he had two rooms adapted for that purpose.

It was soon obvious from the popularity of the classes that the facilities at the Institute were inadequate. But the securing of the Institute for the classes had sown the seed for what was later to develop on the site. Staffordshire County Council, created by the Local Government Act of 1888, had funds ('whisky money') available for technical education. Mr T. Jones, in charge of the County Council department involved, visited Wordsley in 1891 and recommended the building of a new School of Art and Institute as the only way forward to meet adequately the needs of the district. A building committee was formed with Messrs B.F. Mason and W.O. Bowen as honorary joint secretaries. Thomas Robinson of Stourbridge was appointed architect to the project. Other committee members were: Mr J.J. Holbertson, Chairman (on his death the Revd J.J. Slade became Chairman), John Northwood I, and O. Meatyard.

From the architect's plans, Mr Gibbons produced a perspective drawing that headed the subscription list, which was distributed in 1892. Mr F. Stuart of Stuart & Sons Ltd, established glass manufacturers, gave £110 and the Science & Art Department (Government) contributed £348; £275 came in two payments from Staffordshire County Council. About half of the cost of the first part of the scheme, £1,616, came from local contributions. Of the total, £350 was paid to Mr Stuart for the old Institute and site.

Queen Victoria's Diamond Jubilee gave an impetus to the scheme, when it was agreed at a meeting in the National Schools in 1897, chaired by the Rector, that the new Art School would be a suitable monument to commemorate the unique event. This brought in a further donation of £196 from Mr W.H. Richardson. By 1898 matters had progressed to the level at which a stone laying ceremony could be arranged. The building committee met on 24 June 1898 at the National Schools to finalise details of the event, which was held on Monday 27 June. Lieutenant Colonel W.G. Webb JP of Webb's Seeds performed the ceremony and was presented with an inscribed silver trowel. Mr H.G. Richardson provided a bottle, which was used as a time

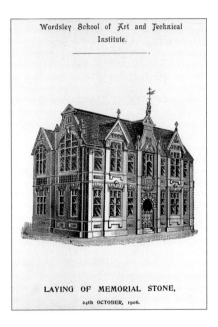

Wordsley School of Art and Technical Institute.

This was the perspective drawing, based on the architect's plan for the project, which was used on the subscription appeal list and distributed in 1892. It was also used in connection with publicity about later events, such as the laying of the memorial stone on 24 October 1906 at the start of the building of the second phase of the work. (*Broadfield House Glass Museum*)

LAYING OF MEMORIAL STONE,
24th OCTOBER, 1906.

capsule, that was buried beneath the foundation stone. The guests later went to the Drill Hall for a concert.

The official opening of the first phase of the project took place on Monday 6 February 1899. Lord Dartmouth, Lord Lieutenant of Staffordshire, opened the building on behalf of the committee and was presented with a silver key by the architect on behalf of the committee. This was followed by lunch in the National Schools, followed by a visit to the Drill Hall for the opening of the associated exhibition. The committee kept alive the idea of completing the building according to the original plans and the funds received a great boost in 1903 with a bequest of £748 from the estate of Mrs Phoebe Carter (formerly Miss Phoebe North of The Cliff). There was a further grant of £554 from Staffordshire County Council and £100 raised locally.

The extension was opened on Monday 16 September 1907 by Alderman J.T. Homer, Chairman of Staffordshire Education Committee. By this time the former enthusiastic chairman had died, so Owen Gibbons CC presided. He was an ideal choice, for it was he who conceived the value of such a school for Wordsley. Many local dignitaries and others were in attendance, including Professor T. Turner, who as a County Council official had been an instigator of the scheme eighteen years previously. The main contractors were Messrs George Meanley & Son, based in Market Street, Kingswinford. Ketley Brick Co. Ltd supplied the bricks, Messrs Harts Hill Iron Co. donated the iron gates for the entrance and Messrs Gibbons & Hinton of Buckpool supplied ornamental tiles. Equipment suppliers included Addison & Co. of Wellington (cupboards and benches), Fisher & Co. of West Bromwich (desks), Gleave & Son of Manchester (benches and tools) and Jabez Attwood (heating system).

There was provision for a weekly attendance of 120 art and science students, 96 handicrafts and 180 cookery students. At the time Wordsley School of Art was regarded as one of the most compact and best-equipped technical institutes in any rural district in the country.

Frederick Carder, born in Brockmoor in 1863 and whose family owned Leys Pottery, an earthenware factory, became a protégé of John Northwood I, works manager and glass designer at Messrs Stevens & Williams of Brierley Hill. Carder lived in John Street, Wordsley, after his marriage. In 1891, in a national art competition, he won his Art Master's Certificate and the Gold Medal of the Year, and became part-time art teacher at Wordsley Art School. In his first year he had 8 students, and five years later, 150. He became Second Master and succeeded Owen Gibbons as Head in 1893.

Disappointed at his prospects at Stevens & Williams after the death of John Northwood I, in 1903 Carder went to Corning, New York, to found the Steuben Glassworks. This was absorbed by Corning Glass in 1917, for which company Carder continued to work until he was 96 years old. He died in 1963, aged 100. *(Broadfield House Glass Museum)*

Owen Gibbons's drawing of the proposed Art School did not include any decorative panels at first-floor level. However, Frederick Carder was invited to design two frontage embellishments for the building. This photograph was taken after the completion of the first phase in 1899. By the time the building was completed in 1907 Frederick was well established at Steuben Glassworks, so his younger brother, George, designed the two matching panels for the second half. *(Broadfield House Glass Museum)*

The terracotta panels at first-floor level. The female figure on the left holding a replica of Northwood's Portland Vase represents Industry. The figure above represents Art. In 1991 in a well-planned raid thieves stole the Carder brothers' panels. They have never been recovered. *(Author's Collection)*

GLASS MANUFACTURE.

A Special Class in this subject is held on Mondays. The Course includes – Composition of Glass generally – Modes of Manufacture – Special properties of Glass – Construction of Furnaces, &c. – Chemical Changes during Manufacture – Composition of Materials used, including colours – Moulds and Tools – Various Methods of Decoration, &c., &c.

The above Syllabus is both *theoretical* and *practical*, and is divided into three grades – Preliminary, Ordinary, and Honours. It is designed to cover the ground of the City and Guilds of London Institute. In the Honours Grade students are expected to possess some knowledge of design, and to attend a class on that subject.

Special attention will be given to Continental methods of work, as studied by the Instructor during the past vacation in Germany and Austria.

Mondays, Preliminary and Ordinary, 7-30 to 9-30.

Honours, 7-30 to 10 p.m.

FEES .. .. .. 2s. 6d.; and Honours, 5s.

Money Prizes, value £4, and Medals are offered by the City and Guilds; and Free Studentships (Money Prizes, value £3, £2, £1), by the Staffs. County Council.

Instructor ... F. CARDER.

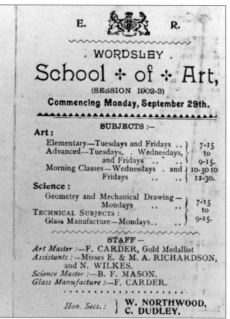

E.   R.

. WORDSLEY .
School ✦ of ✦ Art,
(SESSION 1902-3)

Commencing Monday, September 29th.

SUBJECTS :—

Art :
Elementary — Tuesdays and Fridays .. ⎫ 7·15
Advanced — Tuesdays, . Wednesdays, ⎬ to
and Fridays .. .. ⎭ 9·15.
Morning Classes — Wednesdays . and ⎫ 10-30 to
Fridays .. .. ⎭ 12-30.

Science :
Geometry and Mechanical Drawing — ⎫ 7·15
Mondays .. .. ⎬ to
TECHNICAL SUBJECTS : ⎭
Glass Manufacture — Mondays.. .. 9·15.

STAFF :—
Art Master : — F. CARDER, Gold Medallist
Assistants : — Misses E. & M. A. RICHARDSON, and N. WILKES.
Science Master : — B. F. MASON.
Glass Manufacture : — F. CARDER.

Hon. Secs. : ⎱ W. NORTHWOOD,
⎰ C. DUDLEY.

The prospectus for Wordsley School of Art during Frederick Carder's last year as head, 1902/3. Reference is made to Carder studying in Germany and Austria and the City & Guilds of London Institute, which played an important role in the development of voluntary further education. *(Broadfield House Glass Museum)*

Art students from Wordsley School of Art at Bewdley, early summer 1903. Frederick Carder is seated on the left and to his left is his daughter, Gladys. Behind her on the back row is her mother, Annie, with hands clasped. Also on the back row, sixth from left, is B.F. Mason, head of Brook Street Board School and Honorary Secretary of the Art School Building Committee. Annie died in Corning in 1943. Cyril, son of Frederick and Gladys, a lieutenant serving with US Forces in the First World War, was killed in action in France in July 1918, and Gladys, his sister (Mrs Gladys Welles), died in 1969. Gladys's son, Gillett Welles Jnr, in his eighties in 2000, as the last direct family link with the Carder tomb in Wordsley churchyard, approved the saving of the angel panels. *(Broadfield House Glass Museum)*

Martha Haden Richardson, daughter of
Benjamin Richardson, continued to live
in Wordsley Hall after her father's death
in 1887. She inherited his artistic
interests, was a firm supporter of
Wordsley School of Art and was invited
by the Building Committee to lay the
memorial stone on 24 October 1906 to
mark the completion of the second stage
of the building. Sadly, she contracted
bronchitis in late November 1906 and
died within two weeks, aged 73. She had
been on the local Board of Guardians
and a member of Kingswinford Rural
District Council. Her will made provision
for a charity to benefit 'poor widows over
50 years of age, of good character, not in
receipt of poor relief'. After her death her
brother, William Haden Richardson of
Glasgow, bought the redundant Drill Hall
from the War Office and had it restored
as a public hall, renamed The
Richardson Hall in her memory.
(Broadfield House Glass Museum)

This photograph, taken soon after the completion of the Art School, shows that there was little
variation from the original plans. The school was a Midlands pioneer of voluntary vocational
education. However, the reorganisations of the 1930s made it surplus to requirements, and for
the next forty years it served the village as the base for Wordsley Community Association. This
body outgrew the building and moved to new premises at The Green, Wordsley, in 1975, after
which the Art School was unused and fell into a state of disrepair. As soon as it was announced
that a demolition order on the building had been confirmed because of its dangerous condition,
thieves stole the iron gates. *(Broadfield House Glass Museum)*

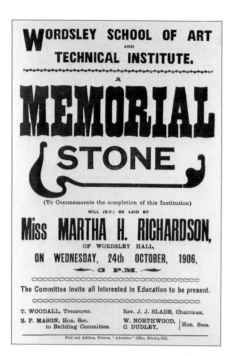

WORDSLEY SCHOOL OF ART
AND
TECHNICAL INSTITUTE.

A

MEMORIAL
STONE

(To Commemorate the completion of this Institution)

WILL (D.V.) BE LAID BY

Miss MARTHA H. RICHARDSON,
OF WORDSLEY HALL,

ON WEDNESDAY, 24th OCTOBER, 1906,

3 P.M.

The Committee invite all interested in Education to be present.

T. WOODALL, Treasurer.	Rev. J. J. SLADE, Chairman.
B. F. MASON, Hon. Sec. to Building Committee.	W. NORTHWOOD, } Hon. Secs. C. DUDLEY, }

Ford and Addison, Printers, "Advertiser" Office, Brierley Hill.

Notification of the completion of a major Wordsley project.
(Ken Rock)

The beginning of the end for an establishment that in the late nineteenth century was a leader in the field of voluntary vocational education. On a wet Sunday in 2000 a JCB is parked ready to start the demolition.
(Author's Collection)

A road on a small housing development off North Street, Brierley Hill, opposite the now derelict Stevens & Williams (Royal Brierley) Glassworks has been named after Frederick Carder. The works where Frederick was a glass designer are awaiting redevelopment by St Mowden Properties.
(Author's Collection)

John Collett, seen here wearing a straw hat, was recruited from Cheltenham's St Paul's Training College for Teachers by the Revd A.G. Girdlestone, curate, to succeed Benjamin Johnson as headmaster of the National School from 1 January 1877. During his forty-four years as headmaster he also held many church offices, including Sunday School superintendent, and was a district councillor on Kingswinford Rural District Council from 1917 to 1929. He died on 6 May 1931 and is buried in Wordsley churchyard. Also in this view, standing third from the left, is teacher John Bailey. *(Author's Collection)*

A 1926 photograph of Standard III, Wordsley Church of England School. Back row, left to right: Gerald Knight, -?-, -?-, Ken Evans, Jim Lees, Bert Moore, Fred Mallen. Middle row: includes Charlie Allcock, Cyril Chamberlain, Arthur Edwards, Vernon Reynolds, Fred Challingsworth. Front row: Dennis Southall, Charlie Rowley, Teddy Baxter, Cliff Nation, -?-, Billy Weaver, -?-. Front row: Harold Jordon, Gordon Warren. *(Wordsley History Society)*

Wordsley C of E School Soccer XI, 1928. Standing, left to right: S. Evans, W. Lees, H. Cartwright, Hodnet, W. Smout, ? Darby, A.E. Edwards. Seated: Eric Edwards, ? Hoult, B. Pardoe, W. Haines, B. Moore. (*Wordsley History Society*)

Standards V and VI, Wordsley C of E School, 1930. Back row, left to right: Don Walton, Bill Lavett, Ron Bills, Geoff Young, Gilbert Pickett, ? Morris, Andrew Phillips. Fourth row: Jack Bailey (teacher), Fred Stevens, Vic Masters, Wilf Evans, Arthur Lowe, Alan Whitehouse, Fred Webb, Ken Evans, Albert Hollis, Bill Taylor. Third row: Fred Bennett, Bill Spears, Fred Willetts, Howard Blanford, Cyril Kinsell, Harry Knight, Bill Goodyear, Ralph Bowater, George Rowbottom, George Webb, Norman Harris, Jack Streak, Cyril Hickman. Second row: Jack Meese, Jack Lamb, Norman Darby, Fred Young, Ernie Bryce. Front row: Tom Weston, Ted Lees, Fred Hall, Herbert Salt, Frank Lowe, Harry Hand, Walter Prescott, Bert Payne, Bill Mortimer, Cecil Cresswell. (*Wordsley History Society*)

Wordsley C of E School Soccer XI, 1931. Standing, left to right: A.E. Ballinger, later headmaster of Brook Street School, Ron Bills, Major Tomlinson, Alan Whitehouse, Bert Payne, Mr Corns. Seated: John Ryder, George Rowbottom, Eric Edwards, Tom Small, Sid Greenaway. Front: Ernie Bryce, Gilbert Pickett, Herbert Salt. *(Wordsley History Society)*

A class from Wordsley C of E School, 1933. Back row, left to right: Bill Matcroft, ? Yates, Bill Wassell, Dennis Lichfield, Ray Breese, ? Greenaway, Bill Spears, Fred Postins, Richard Powell. Third row: Ray Fawdry, George Elwell, Sampson Mansell, Jack Everes, Chris Murray, ? Ball, Sid Howell, ? Perry, George Bills, Bill Lewis. Second row: Jack Pardoe, ? Pearce, Harry Cooper, Walter Salt, ? Darby, Albert Foster, ? Bryce, Jack Bennett, Jack Turley, David Smith, Bill Walker. Front row: Don Fasey, Ray Jeavons, ? Smart, Len Poulton, Bert Payne, Bob Lees, Jim Reynolds. *(Wordsley History Society)*

The opening ceremony for the new Kingswinford Board School in Brook Street, Wordsley, was held on 10 November 1884 with Benjamin F. Mason as headmaster. He had opened the original school in the Wesleyan Methodist Chapel in Brettell Lane under Kingswinford School Board on 21 August 1882. Within a year, on 21 June 1883, the school managers met to select a site for a new school to be built at Audnam. The original school closed on 7 November 1884. (*Author's Collection*)

Brook Street Board School, 1887. The children are dressed up as workers in various occupations and industries during a Queen Victoria's Golden Jubilee celebratory event at the school, which included two performances of a dramatic cantata. The central figure, John Bull, was probably B.F. Mason, headmaster from 1882 to 1922. Joseph Henry Haden, front row, fifth from left and dressed in a shepherd's hat and smock, was born in Chapel Street in 1880 and later lived in Alwen Street. He became a pupil teacher and obtained a Queen's Scholarship in 1898 to train as a teacher at Bangor Normal College. He returned to teach in Wordsley. He was the grandfather of the late Mrs Beryl Bromley of Bridgnorth. (*Mrs Beryl Bromley*)

These two early twentieth-century views of classes at Brook Street both show headmaster B.F. Mason and the class teacher. Both boards proclaim 'Wordsley Council School' for Staffordshire County Council, established in 1888, which had assumed responsibility for the former Kingswinford Board Schools. The mixed class is dated March 1906, the boys' class is undated but from about the same period. The children's attire suggests that they had been warned of the photographer's visit and were in their Sunday best. *(Frank Power)*

'Wordsley Council School Football Team 1921' says the board. Standing in the middle, back row, is B.F. Mason (headmaster). The only other person identified is John Shillingford, seated, centre. He was selected to play for England Schoolboys, but his mother insisted that he started his apprenticeship in glass decorating at Richardsons, which coincided with the football 'call-up', so he did not play. He later played in the Stourbridge and District Church and Chapel League for Amblecote Wesleyan Football Club whose ground was at Box Hill, Wordsley, and for other teams until he was forty years old. He died aged 93. *(Mrs Catherine Wood)*

The 1975 cup-winning rounders team. Back row, left to right: Kevin Gripton, -?-, -?-, George Hodgson (headmaster), Chris Batson, Neil Sayce, Peter Shillingford, S. George Yardley (deputy head). Front row: Frankie Jones, -?-, Nigel ?, Errol Shillingford, -?-. *(Mrs L. Yardley)*

In September 1972 the Brook Primary School was relocated in the former Audnam Secondary School buildings under George Hodgson's headmastership, with fourteen teachers. Mr Hodgson became Dudley's Religious Education Adviser in 1979 and George Yardley, deputy head, who had been on the staff since 1950, became head for the last year of his service, retiring in July 1980. Seen here with 11–12 year old pupils are S. George, Yardley, Peggy Nash who retired in 1981, and Kevin Gripton, deputy head, who became head of Bromley Hills Primary School. (*Mrs L. Yardley*)

A selection of the sixty 11–12-year-old pupils who staged a musical about Queen Elizabeth I and William Shakespeare, April 1981. The script was written by Kevin Gripton, deputy head, who augmented original Shakespearian prose with a smattering of local humour and dialect. There were full houses for three performances and the proceeds were shared by the Church of England's Children's Society and the school fund. (*Stourbridge News Incorporating County Express*)

Two long-serving teachers retired in July 1980. Front row, left to right: Margaret Goby, S. George Yardley (acting headmaster). Children standing include Vicki Jordan, Marie Saunders, Anne Kimberley, -?-, -?-, Andrew Longville, Scott Whapples, -?-. (*Stourbridge News Incorporating County Express*)

In its centenary year, 1982, the school had a carnival float as part of the Brook School Fayre. Adults helping included, left to right, Marjorie Dalwood (caretaker, back row, fourth from left), and a group of three ladies, top right: Pat Banner, Wyn Ratcliffe, Josie Bunn. (*Stourbridge News Incorporating County Express*)

Lawnswood Road School was opened in 1912 by Staffordshire County Council to serve the growing population of the village. This 1939 scene shows the May Queen and her attendants. Paul Husselbee is the only boy. The others include Joyce Rowbottom (May Queen), Hilda Phillips, Freda Woodward, Jean Foster and Valerie Cook. *(Wordsley History Society)*

Two milk monitors at Lawnswood School wheeling the school's milk delivery from the school gate towards the classrooms, late 1960s. Milk was supplied to schools from the 1930s when one-third pint bottles were available to pupils for ½d. This was to aid childhood nutrition and struggling farmers. In the 1940s it was made available to all children free of charge. A standard routine developed in schools: collection by class monitor of the appropriate number of bottles a few minutes before morning break, distribution of straws, careful punching of the cardboard disk bottle tops and, after drinking, collection of the empties, straws and tops. Distribution of free milk in schools for the over sevens ceased in 1971 during a government economy drive. The last free milk for five to seven year olds ended in 1980. It is still available for a small charge. *(Wordsley History Society)*

Despite having limited sports facilities, Lawnswood School participated fully in various area league programmes. This is the 1966/7 Netball Team. *(Wordsley History Society)*

To reduce travelling for inter-schools games, schools on the western edge of the borough had their own league, the County League. Lawnswood Primary School won the league football competition in the 1968/9 season and were also the Campbell Cup finalists. Standing, left to right: I.G. Lewis (teacher), M. Curtis, R. Clarke, A. Chilton, M. Buckingham, P. Wassell, M. Kinsella (headmaster). Seated: includes T. Parfitt, A. Downton, R. Keeley, P. Hudson. *(Wordsley History Society)*

Lawnswood Road Primary School Rounders Team 1968/9. Standing, left to right: Mrs D.G. Lythall, P. Pritchard, J. Reynolds, H. Dimmock, L. Attwood, M. Baker, M. Kinsella (headmaster). Seated: R. John, E. Cull, L. Martin, C. Bird, P. Hudson. (*Wordsley History Society*)

The skittleball team of 1968/9. Standing, left to right: includes J. Mallen, Mrs D.G. Lythall, S. Goldsby, E. Cull, M. Baker, P. Hudson, M. Kinsella (headmaster), J. Kings. Seated: H. Dimmock, C. Dews, L. Martin, C. Bird, L. Attwood. (*Wordsley History Society*)

Belle Vue Infants' School was the first post-Second World War school to be built in Wordsley to meet the needs of the rapidly expanding population, which by 1966 had grown to 18,000 and three years later to 21,500. Built for an intake of 80 pupils a year, it was officially opened by Alderman J.T. Wilson on 1 December 1967, some months after coming into use. The photograph is of the staff at the first money-raising event, a harvest festival. Seated: Iris Gill (headmistress), Brenda Kent (deputy head), D. Skelding; standing: P. Stanton, Ann Wood. *(Mrs I. Gill)*

Some junior children were accommodated in the infants' school for a short time, nominally on Lawnswood Road School's roll but for practical purposes under Mrs Gill's care. These pupils moved into the new junior school when it was ready. Similarly, until Ashwood Park School was ready children destined for that school were accommodated temporarily. The combined staff at Christmas 1971 are shown here. Standing, left to right: includes Vera Simpson, Pat Lintern, Sonia Hingley, Susan Wars, Janice Williams, Denise Horton, Irene Siviter. Seated: Anne Cooper, Laura Dixon, Brenda Kent, Iris Gill, Pat Stanton, Dorothy Stevens, Marjorie Roberts. *(Mrs I. Gill)*

Belle Vue Junior School was officially opened on 22 November 1968 by Councillor D. Harty, with Edric Pearson as headmaster. The school cost over £80,000 and was designed for 320 children of 7–11 years of age. The infants' and junior schools were amalgamated on the retirement of Mrs I. Gill in 1984. A nursery department was added in 1986, and on Mr Pearson's retirement in August 1988 there were 450 children in 14 classes in the amalgamated extended school. The photograph shows the junior school staff at the opening in 1968. Left to right: Edric Pearson, Dorothy Sutton, Gill Broadbent, Sue Smith, Ethel Hough (school secretary). *(Edric Pearson)*

A late 1960s school ritual: children say prayers before drinking their free milk. *(Edric Pearson)*

In 1974/5 the school soccer XI became the league champions and six of them won the Dudley 6-a-side competition. Standing, left to right: B. Ellerton (teacher), Philip Whitticase, Jonathan Wright, Martin Cox, M. Dunn, Mark Bradley, Stuart Parry, Andrew Ensor. Front row: David Sutton, Stuart Clark, Paul Whitticase, Michael Raybone, Andrew Wilkinson, Christopher Noakes. *(Edric Pearson)*

This was the 1975 Belle Vue Junior School Netball Team, which won the league. Julia Crighton was the teacher in charge. *(Edric Pearson)*

This was Class L in 1977. Back row, left to right: E. Pearson (headmaster), -?-, -?-, -?-, -?-, Jonathan Wright, Graham Nunn (deputy head and year co-ordinator). Middle row: Carl Bridgwater, -?-, Arthur Rudge, -?-, Oliver ?, Stuart Clarke, -?-, John Baggott, Jimmy Ross, Mark Whitticase. Front row: Julie ?, -?-, -?-, Andrea Wallis, Amanda Hill, Susan Fox, Pat Lucas (teacher), Julie ?, -?-, Karen Wheeler, Melanie Pitt, Rowena Clarke. *(Edric Pearson)*

The first headteachers of the Belle Vue Schools, Edric Pearson (1968–88) and Mrs Iris Gill (1967–84). During their headships age ranges varied: five to seven, five to eight (infants), seven to eleven, eight to twelve (juniors). It is now a three to eleven primary school. *(Edric Pearson)*

Fairhaven Primary School, built on land off Barnett Lane and opened in 1969, was the second post-Second World War school to serve Wordsley. This was the original staff. Standing, left to right: Gwen Nottingham, Mary Wilson. Seated: V. Clarke (school secretary), Brian Pinches (headmaster), Eileen Bailey, B. Cloke. (*John Dallaway*)

By 1975 the staff had grown considerably. Back row, left to right: -?-, -?-, -?-, V. Clarke (school secretary), -?-, -?-, A. Turley, P. Barber. Front row: -?-, E. Bailey, Trevor Taylor (deputy head), B. Pinches (headmaster), B. Cloke, -?-, M. Wilson. (*Mrs Eileen Bailey*)

The 1979 Under XI soccer team. Back row, left to right: B. Pinches (headmaster), Neil Griffiths, A. Taylor, Charles Johnson, P. Jeram (teacher), Andrew Bullingham, -?-, Chris Woods, P. Barber. Front row: -?-, Mark Yardley, -?-, -?-, Martin Roach, Chris Norris. *(John Dallaway)*

The 1983 cricket team with their teachers. Standing, left to right: J. Dallaway (teacher), Andrew Merman, Simon Pittaway, Matthew Mannings, Dean Clifford, A. Shirodkar, A. Perigo (teacher). Front row: Andrew Griffiths, Paul Jones, Lee Thacker, Andrew Cox, Satyen Desai. *(John Dallaway)*

The 1983 rounders team. Back row, left to right: -?-, Jennifer Baker, Alison Eley. Middle row: Ruth Powell, Joanne Benham, Joanne Hopkins, Helen Bayley. Front row: Victoria Grainger, Claire Powell, Linda Potter, E. Lowe (teacher), Nicola Williams. *(John Dallaway)*

The table tennis team, 1984. Back row, left to right: Andrew Skelding, Philip Lucas (headmaster), Andrew Griffiths, Matthew Mannings. Seated: Dean Clifford, Claire Powell, Andrew Cox. *(John Dallaway)*

In November 1983 a well-wisher at Ashwood School organised a helicopter trip for a sick child at the school. Accompanied by representatives from several classes, he was given this treat by well-known Brierley Hill businessman Anthony Whittaker who flies his own helicopter from Halfpenny Green. Anthony really made it a memorable experience for his passengers, for he flew the small party to the Stone Manor Hotel, near Kidderminster, for lunch. The helicopter is seen here near the school; Mrs J. Wakefield (headmistress) is on the right. *(Susan Wright)*

Ashwood School often prepared floats for Wordsley Carnival. In June 1985 Red Indians were the theme. *(Susan Wright)*

To mark the twenty-fifth anniversary of the school, an extension to the library was opened, 26 June 1995. In the centre is Trevor Taylor (headmaster), who retired in July 2004. *(Susan Wright)*

When the school library was opened a balloon race was staged. Mr Taylor is in the middle directing the release of the balloons. *(Susan Wright)*

Audnam Senior School, George Street, Wordsley, opened in 1938 under the headmastership of Frederick Dale who had been a Minor Counties cricketer. The school was one of six built in the former Brierley Hill Urban District area in the 1930s to cater for 11–14 year olds. There was soon a change of headmaster. J. Arthur Bradley, headmaster of Bent Street Senior Boys' School, Brierley Hill, took charge from 1939. This was the staff in about 1940. Standing, left to right: Mary Owen, Wilf Guttery (later deputy head), L. Perry, Miss Spicer, C.W. Hill, Frank Holmshaw (later head of Wall Heath C of E School). Seated: Albert Solomon Moreton (pupil teacher 1899–1903, woodwork master, retired in 1948), Esme Allen (became a headteacher), J.A. Bradley, -?-, Reg Corns. *(Author's Collection)*

Audnam Secondary School Cricket XI won the area schools' knock-out competition on the Labour-in-Vain ground, Brockmoor, soundly beating Brierley Hill Grammar School, in July 1950. Standing, left to right: L.J. Roberts (teacher), Terry Harris, Jeff Southall, Bert Wooley, Brian Stelmack, Stanley Hall, Stan Hill (teacher and author). Seated: Peter Jeavons, Clifford Barras, Victor Sneyd, Tom Beckley (captain), Geoffrey Freeman, William Harper, Brian Cadman. Stanley Hall was the star of the match, taking 10 wickets and scoring 69 runs. *(Author's Collection)*

In the 1950s Staffordshire Education Committee was progressive in its support for schools. A very active Physical Education Department was directed by Amos Breese supported by divisional organisers. Camp craft courses for teachers were organised before they took their school parties for a week at one of the county camps. Audnam School took advantage of this provision each year. Here the twenty-eight campers are having a meal in a marquee at the Beaudesert camp near Cannock Chase, in the early 1950s. Staff in charge, left to right: Stan Hill, Olaf, a Swedish student engaged for the summer term, and R.A. Sweeting. *(Author's Collection)*

Stan Walker of Stourbridge was for several years the camp warden at Beaudesert. Here, he lived the life of a backwoodsman during the summer, his accommodation being a tepee. He instructed visiting groups in camp craft and country lore. Part of the programme was a 10-mile hike over Cannock Chase. Here an Audnam party is seen assembled in wet weather about to set off, with teachers Stan Hill and R.A. Sweeting in charge. *(Author's Collection)*

Audnam School pupils visited the Houses of Parliament in 1952. Back row: includes Stan Hill (teacher), Y. Francis, R. Bower, Tom Johnson, R. Quarrington, Terry Harris, R.A. Sweeting (teacher), Jim Simmons MP, George Dodd, J.A. Bradley (headmaster), George Wigg MP, L.J. Roberts, Norma Dodd. Second row: includes Bob Gregg, Michael Harper, Hazel Darrie, Judith and Janet Edgerton, Janet Henley, Pat Priest, Pat Turner. Front row: includes Gwenda Zinke, Mary Fones, Jill Cardoe, Jill Brockhouse. *(Author's Collection)*

Class 4A in 1954. Back row, left to right: John Mills, -?-, -?-, -?-, -?-, -?-, -?-, -?-. Front row: Janet Oakley, Betty Fenn, Ann Sidaway, Janet Southall, Hilary Bourne, Pat Clarke, Stan Hill (teacher), -?-, Ann Hillman, Margaret Sayce, Diane Stevens, Linda Cartwright, Jean Masters. First row standing: -?-, Wendy Hart, Barbara Bennett, Maureen Bills, Pat Clarke, Joyce Dickens, -?-, Barbara Humphries, Joan Richardson, Bridget Hudson, -?-, Pamela Pearce, -?-, -?-, Barbara Tolley, Joan Mallin, -?-. Second row standing: Tony Thompson, Melvin Price, Michael Greenaway, Colin Boden, Peter Cartwright, Peter Devereux, Edward Woods, Alan Simpson, Tony Butcher, John Webb. There were forty-five pupils in the class. *(Author's Collection)*

Class 4A in 1956. Front row, left to right: Kathleen Southall, Gillian Beddard, Diane Pardoe, Carol Cartwright, -?-, Stan Hill (teacher), Patricia Smith, -?-, Susan Pinches, Iris Simpson, Maureen Ballinger. Second row: Ken Banks, Eileen Caddick, Christine Smart, Brenda Hughes, Pauline Hill, -?-, -?-, -?-, Pat Morgan, Betty Harvey, Hazel Darrie, Brian Bridge. Third row: David Davies, Arthur Jones, Dennis Curtis, Norman Shillingford, -?-, Robert Williams, Alan Pilkington, Peter Bradley, Fred Harris, Alf Woods. Back row: John Emery, Clive Carter, Arnold Hayden, Joe Jones, Eric Smith, -?-. *(Author's Collection)*

Class 4A in 1957. Front row, left to right: Barry Allen, John Jasper, Michael Biddlecombe, Peter Burke, Dave Cartwright, Stan Hill (teacher), Janice Goodall, Margaret Phillips, Daline Thomas, Joan Bedford, Barbara Saunders. Second row: Frank Cogzel, Rita Cooper, Roy Mason, Eric Longville, Graham Young, June Wootton, -?-, Barbara Mason, Mavis Hill, Maureen Bennett. Third row: Joan Phillips, Janet Oakley, June Ridler, Tina Randle, Carol Harper, Frances Mackenzie, Brenda Venables, Janet Malpass, Betty Southall, Ann Page. Back row: George Higgs, Dennis Wentworth, Geoffrey Barnsley, -?-, David Porter, Cyril Gallier, Raymond Kidd, Frank Bullock. *(Author's Collection)*

During the 1950s the school staged an annual December operetta produced and directed by Norma Dodd. These shows involved a large number of children on stage and in the supporting choir, making costumes, scenery and painting backcloths. The principals in the 1957 performance were, left to right, fourth along: George Dodd, a fine baritone whose support was invaluable, Diane Crutchley, Dave Cartwright, Barbara Saunders, Geoffrey Barnsley, -?-, Daline Thoms. *(Author's Collection)*

Audnam School's Woodwork Department under Joseph Taylor undertook a number of constructions on which boys could work when they had acquired sufficient skill in the craft. These projects involved building a small fleet of canoes, a chicken and battery hen unit, garden shed, planters and so on. Here is the team that built a substantial greenhouse in the early 1950s. Left to right: Barry Pilkington, G. Husselbee, Trevor Taylor, Trevor Watts, -?-, Brian Underhill, William Harper, B. Nicklin, Clive Carter, Kenneth Grainger, Roger Mills. *(Pearl Taylor)*

Audnam School became the Brierley Hill Soccer League Champions at the end of the 1957/8 season. Back row, left to right: G. Barnsley, D. Cartwright, K. Cotterill, Stan Hill (teacher), F. Gregg, ? Wale, M. Harvey, M. Cotterill. Front row: R. Hill, E. Longville, ? Bishop (captain), ? Southall, ? Green. *(Author's Collection)*

Audnam Secondary School pupils had the choice of many extra-curricular activities in which to participate in the second half of the twentieth century. There were many enthusiastic members of staff to encourage pupils in sports, drama, music, and to organise excursions. The school participated in Dudley LEA-led cruises in 1970 and 1972. These girls on the September/October 1970 cruise to Morocco, Spain and Portugal were snapped on deck. *(Wolverhampton Express & Star)*

Led by Mrs J. Price and Mr J. Taylor in 1970 the thirty-one-strong group were Ian and Martin Allen, Susan Bailey, Janet Bradley, Kevin Brooks, Lynne Buckingham, Kim Cook, Diane Craye, Michael Davies, Lorraine Edge, Leslie Hanbury, Jane Hartshorne, Ann Hewitt, Stephen Hill, Maureen Hingley, Michael Jones, Susan Leech, David Lewis, Yvonne Longmore, Martyn Penn, Alison Parkes, David Rakowski, Denise Raybould, Debra Richardson, Stephen Skeldon, Jane Stephens, Andrea Timmins, Tracey Wakefield, Vanessa Walker, Linda Woodcock. (*Wolverhampton Express & Star*)

A vigorous programme of activities was arranged to occupy pupils on the voyages between ports of call. Here four girls are enjoying a dip in the deck swimming pool. Mr J. Taylor is in attendance. (*Wolverhampton Express & Star*)

Many photographs were taken by the pupils to record an adventure abroad, which was not commonplace in the 1970s. Here fifteen girls of the party are snapped on deck. *(Wolverhampton Express & Star)*

Another smaller party went on a similar cruise in 1972, again with Mr Taylor as leader: Susan Bailey, Mandy Baker, Susan Collett, Julie Devis, Jane Doyle, Lynn Dunn, Jane Egan, Shirley Elcock, Susan Skeldon, Davina Smith, Mandy Stanton and Elaine Walker; and five boys: Robert Bradley, John Blackham, Tony Curtis, David Jesson, Kevin Phipson. *(Pearl Taylor)*

This fine new school on the edge of the Dingle on Brierley Hill Road was opened in 1972 by Dudley Education Authority to replace Audnam Secondary School, built at the top of George Street in 1938/9. The staff and pupils of the latter transferred to the new building. First named the Buckpool School, this was changed recently to the Wordsley School. *(Author's Collection)*

Two long-serving teachers retired in 1980, George Dodd (left) and Joseph Taylor. Their wives Norma Dodd (left) and Pearl Taylor accompanied them at their retirement party. *(Stourbridge News Incorporating County Express)*

Form 3M1 in 1980. Front row, left to right: -?-, Cheri Jones-Cooper, -?-, Joanne Rock, -?-, Sandra Longville, Michelle Platman, -?-, -?-. Second row: Wayne Morris, Neil Marsh, Melanie Smith, Anna Scott, -?-, -?-, Rebecca Hemming, Mark Southall, Ian Hayden. Third row: Glen Johnson, -?-, Andrew Wood, Paul Field, Simon Barney, Alan Guest, David Ellis, Andrew Pilkington. Back row: Craig Bevan, Richard Taylor, Ross Wheeler. *(Alan Pilkington)*

Form 4-3 in 1981. Front row, left to right: -?-, -?-, Melanie Smith, Joanne Rock, Miss Spittle, Rebecca Hemming, -?-, -?-, -?-. Middle row: Ian Hayden, Andrew Pilkington, Sandra Longville, -?-, Simon Barney, -?-, Michelle Platman, David Ellis, Mark Southall. Back row: Glenn Johnson, Alan Guest, Craig Bevan, Richard Taylor, Andrew Wood, Neil Shillingford, Neil March, Wayne Morris. *(Alan Pilkington)*

Form 2A in 1985. Front row: Lisa Shillingford, Sharon Bradley, Sharon Simmonds, Donna Hartshorne, Andrea Liddell, Karen Jones, Sally Bowater, Claire Kelly, Dawn Skidmore. Middle row: Carl Pullen, Mark Andrews, Geoff Murphy, Lee Brown, Kay Harris, Lee Proudler, Stuart Baggott, Mark Grigg, Stephen Pilkington. Back row: Tim Harris, Ian Bissell, Stephen Saunders, Ian Hodkiss, Michael Day, Richard Wood. *(Alan Pilkington)*

Form 3BG in 1986. Front row, left to right: Dawn Skidmore, Sharon Simmonds, Kay Harris, Mr Dickenson, Donna Hartshorne, Andrea Liddell, Claire Kelly. Middle row: Mark Andrews, Richard Wood, Stuart Baggott, Karen Jones, Lisa Shillingford, Michael Day, Lee Proudler, Stephen Pilkington. Back row: Mark Grigg, Ian Bissell, Ian Hodgkiss, Stephen Saunders, Tim Harris, Lee Brown, Carl Pullen. *(Alan Pilkington)*

7

Leisure & Community

Wordsley
Amateur Dramatic & Operatic Society
(August 1924)

WILL PRESENT

Tilly of Bloomsbury
(IAN HAY)

by kind permission of

Messrs. S. FRENCH & SONS (London)

Wordsley
Amateur Dramatic & Operatic Society
(August 1924)

—— WILL PRESENT ——

Tilly of Bloomsbury
(IAN HAY)

by kind permission of
Messrs. S. FRENCH & SONS (London)

AT

"OLYMPIA," Wordsley,

ON

Wednesday, September 30th, 1925

Doors open 7 p.m.
Commence 7-30 p.m.

Tickets - 1/6, 1/-, (including tax)
and 6d.

President:
REV. R. H. FOWLER.

Vice=Presidents:
REV. R. H. WYATT,   E. W. HATTON, Esq.

Hon. Sec. & Treasurer:
S. EVANS, Esq.

Costumiere:
Mrs. F. WHITNEY.

Actor Manager:
H. SUTTON, Esq.

Committee:
The above, with
Miss N. MILLS,
Mr. G. RELF.

Previous Production:
"East Lynne"—February 1925.

CAST in order of appearance.

Abel Mainwaring, M.P.	Mr. W. E. Brookes
Milroy (a Butler)	Mr. G. Relf
Sylvia (Mainwaring's Daughter)	Miss N. Mills
Lady Marian Mainwaring	Miss M. Newnam
Rev. Adrian Rylands	Mr. S. Evans
Constance Damer	Miss J. Brookes
Richard (Mainwaring's Son)	Mr. H. Sutton
Tilly (Welwyn's Daughter)	Miss F. Hickman
Percy („ Son)	Mr. G. Wall
Amelia („, younger daughter)	Miss A. I. Skelding
Grandma Banks	Miss J. Brookes
Mr. Metha Ram (a Law Student)	Mr. S. Evans
Mrs. Welwyn	Miss K. Cartwright
Lucius Welwyn	Mr. G. Relf
Mr. Stillbottle (Sheriff's Officer)	Miss I. Baker
Mr. Pumpherston (A Law Student)	Mr. H. Druce

Synopsis of Scenery.

Act 1.
The Towers,   A Saturday Afternoon
  Shotley Beauchamp.   November

Act 11.
The Welwyns' Drawing Room,   Monday
  Bloomsbury   Afternoon

Act 111.
Same as Act 11.   Tuesday Morning
——MODERN DRESS.——

Wordsley Amateur Dramatic Society (WADS) was founded by Horace Sutton in 1924 as the Wordsley Amateur Dramatic and Operatic Society. Associated with him as actor-manager were Sidney Evans (hon. secretary and treasurer), G. Rolf, Nellie Bowater and Miss N. Mills. *East Lynne* by Mrs Henry Wood, performed in the Richardson Hall in February 1925, was their first play. This programme was for the second play and records a move to the Olympia Cinema. Officials then included the Revd R.H. Fowler (Rector 1923–60), E.W. Hatton (National School headmaster), and Mrs F. Whitney (costumier, of the Wordsley drapery and clerical outfitting business). Other plays followed, including *Eliza Comes to Stay* and *The Private Secretary*. (Bob Cotton)

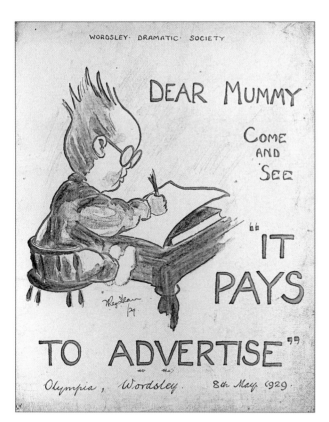

These charming, simple advertisements were designed by Reg Dean. Charles Hatton produced plays for a time and was succeeded in 1935 by D.R. Guttery, a Brierley Hill schoolmaster, later well known as a local historian. During the Second World War Bill Swaithes, a Dudley Technical College lecturer, kept the society active with play readings and the production of one-act plays. *(Bob Cotton)*

The cast for a play in 1949. Back row, left to right: John Symonds (community centre warden), Nellie Bowater (Brook Street schoolteacher), -?-, Frank Dillon. Front row: Betty Mulcahy (member 1948–50, later broadcaster and elocutionist), John Evers, Gwen Low, Peggy Wall. *(Bob Cotton)*

In 1958 *The Reluctant Debutante* was performed. Standing left to right: John Smith, Una Payton, Percy Oakley (community centre warden), Frank Dillon, Moya Dillon, Stanley Jones. Seated: Brenda Richards and Bob Wall. *(Bob Cotton)*

Another 1958 production was *The Sacred Flame*. Standing, left to right: Mary Drinkwater, Percy Oakley, Bob Wall, John Smith, Betty Mulcahy, Graham Bennett, Una Payton. Seated: Kim Drinkwater, Bob Wood, Brenda Richards, Nellie Bowater, Norman Wilkes. *(Bob Cotton)*

WADS members, mid-1970s. Standing, left to right: Eve Bartram, Bob Cotton, Margaret Walden, Freddie Walden, Margaret Kennedy, Jeff Kennedy, John Mahony, Pam Keely, Alan Jones, Sue Mead. Front row: Olive Luckhurst, June Head, Sharon Whittaker, Hazel Poole, Dink Widdowson, Jill Bennett. *(Bob Cotton)*

In October 1979 *Hay Fever* was performed with, left to right, Dink Widdowson, Stuart Robertson, Bob Cotton, Margaret Walden, holding the *Express & Star* Trophy (a top award for Midlands amateur dramatic societies), Jill Bennett, Sally Cotton, Martin Whittaker, June Head. *(Bob Cotton)*

Lloyd George Knew My Father was performed in October 1980. Cast, left to right: Bill Weston, Dink Widdowson, Stuart Robertson, Steve Fletcher, Sally Cotton. Seated: Bob Cotton, Margaret Walden. *(Bob Cotton)*

During its eighty-year existence WADS has performed in the Richardson Hall, the Olympia Cinema, the former Wordsley School of Art (community centre), and since 1967 Stream Road Methodist Church Hall. Until the mid-1930s live music was performed at each production. At the performance of *The Farmer's Wife* in 1930, music was provided by four violins, two violas, two cellos and a piano. In 1931, an unsuccessful attempt was made to use a radio-gramophone. Now a modern sound reproduction system is used.

Following in the steps of Charles Hatton, actor/producer member Andrew Rock wrote *Answers on a Postcard*, which WADS has performed three times. Altogether some 160 plays have been presented, most of them 'three acts'. Since 1970 many awards have been won, including, in the Wolverhampton Drama Federation, 9 Best Production, 13 Production, 14 Best Actor/Actress, 4 Set, 4 Supporting; and in One-Act Festivals: 8 Best Production, 1 Production, 7 Best Actor/Actress.

The Society has contributed greatly to the social life of the district and is recognised as one of its leading amateur dramatic groups.

Many community centres were set up after the First World War to bring to new housing estates amenities that people were used to as part of the life of established towns. Since those early days community centres have spread throughout the country and play an important part in the social life of the district served.

This publicity shot was taken on the Great Pool at Himley Hall to advertise the 1988 production of *On Golden Pond*. Left to right: Jill Bennett, Bob Cotton, Tim Harrington. *(Bob Cotton)*

Lives and Luxury was produced in May 1971. Cast, standing, left to right: Jill Bennett, Bob Cotton, Shirley Bough. Seated: Margaret Claridge, Dink Widdowson. *(Bob Cotton)*

   In Wordsley the Art School closed in 1938, its technical instruction being offered in more modern institutions elsewhere. During the Second World War the building had several uses. The establishment of the Wordsley Council of Social Service was an important step, and the Women's Club was the first lasting group to be formed to use the redundant premises. From 1941 when W. Bennett became warden, the activities on offer there increased rapidly. In 1941 the Duke of Kent came to the centre to visit the Women's Club. This event was said to be the first visit by royalty since the fleeting visit by Charles II in September 1651, after the battle of Worcester. Staffordshire Education Authority paid for the part-time instructors and staff; these responsibilities were assumed by Dudley Education Authority after the 1966 Local Government reorganisation. Major William Harcourt-Webb, of the famous firm of seedsmen, was the first President of the Community Association and he was succeeded in 1952 by A. Norman Piddock. By the 1960s the old building could not cope adequately with the needs of the thriving Community Association and eventually the new building at Wordsley Green was built.

At the Community Association Annual Dinner and Dance at the Stewpony Hotel, 15 February 1967, the special guests were Mr J. Clement Jones (editor of the *Express & Star*) and his wife. Left to right: Barbara Davies, Mrs Valerie Radford (chairman of the Flower Arranging Group), Mr H. Sutton (chairman), Mr J. Clement Jones, Dr Bartlett (president), Mrs Clement Jones. *(Wolverhampton Express & Star)*

The Lively Ladies is a long-established group at Wordsley Community Centre. Those attending enjoy a range of activities including talks, demonstrations, visits and meals out. These ladies are demonstrating elaborate hats in the 1966 Easter Bonnet Parade. Standing, left to right: Margaret Thomas, Barbara Colquet, -?-, -?-. Seated: Nellie Evans, Joyce Perry, Pam Brettell. *(Stourbridge News Incorporating County Express)*

A table of Lively Ladies at the Himley House Hotel for a Christmas meal, *c.* 1970. Left to right: -?-, Mary Smart, -?-, Jean Hill, Doreen Keay, Jean Morris. *(Author's Collection)*

At this 1960s dancing class were, left to right Mr Mills, Mrs Phillips, Joe Edwards, Mrs Mills, Mrs Grainger, Stan Grainger and Jack Haden of the *County Express* making notes for a report. Mr and Mrs Mills ran the classes. *(Stourbridge News Incorporating County Express)*

The Friendly Club, 1980 – not a man in sight. *(Stourbridge News Incorporating County Express)*

Refreshment provision was always important; these ladies acted as servers in the 1960s. Left to right: June Randle, Mrs Randle, Miss Randle, Mrs Stokes, Mrs May Pitt. *(Wordsley History Society)*

These ladies were regular attenders at the old Community Centre. The group includes Mrs Millward, Mrs Challingsworth, Mrs Abbot, Jennie Facer, Elsie Waltier. *(Wordsley History Society)*

In 1952 the Carnival Queen was Nancy Smith, who is seen here addressing the crowd. F.J. Symonds (community centre warden) is holding the microphone. *(Wordsley History Society)*

Another of the 1952 Wordsley Carnival events was the bowls competition. Here the Carnival Queen, Nancy Smith, has just presented the prizes to the winners, Herbert Price and George Smith, with many bowls club members in attendance. *(Wordsley History Society)*

Winners of the Wordsley Carnival Tennis Competition and committee members. Standing, left to right: Joe Lees, Norman Humpage, -?-, -?-, -?-, Harry Ryder, -?-, Geoff Whitworth. Seated: Olwyn Timmins, Carnival Queen Nancy Smith, John Ryder. (*Wordsley History Society*)

The 1966 Wordsley Gala Queen and her attendants. (*Stourbridge News Incorporating County Express*)

Wordsley events were always well attended. In 1930 'Sporty' Matthews assembled over sixty children for his 'jazz' band, all equipped with their 'buzzers', one step up from tissue paper and comb. *(Wordsley History Society)*

Wordsley Olympic Football Team played on a soccer pitch on Fox Hill before moving to Wordsley Sports Club, situated on the site of the present Graham Road. Back row, left to right: H. Hatton, J. Powell, C. Randle, C. Bowater. Middle row, standing: H. Attwood, S. Grainger, A. Jones, S. Thompson, A. Haines, J. Price (trainer). Seated: L. Newman, C. Rowbottom, H. Sutton, H. Wilkes, W. Slater (captain), W. Evans, E. Thompson, W. Nicholls. On the ground: S. Perks, B. Baker. The team's successes included winners of Cradley Heath & District League Division III and Junior Cup, and runner up in the Griffin Shield. *(Wordsley History Society)*

Wordsley Boys' Club Soccer Team winners of the Brierley Hill Youth League Championship, 1948/9 season, outside Wordsley Conservative Club. Standing, left to right: Stan Grainger, Bob Sheriff, Mike Harris, Billy Jones, Bob Firmstone, Frank Randle, Tom Farmer, Ken Hall, Arthur Bridges (leader). Seated: Tony Harris, Les James, Peter Lyth, Harold Payne, Horace Hickman, Geoff Knott, Reg Poole. *(Mike Harris)*

Sixteen-year-old Anita Stevens of Tack Farm Road, Wordsley, a member of the 4th Wordsley Guides, at their meeting venue, Fairhaven School, was presented with the Queen's Award, the first member of her company to achieve it, February 1979. In the build-up to the award she acquired many badges, including one for camp craft and another for a project studying the lifestyles of members of the Commonwealth. Left to right: Mary Harris (commissioner), Jennifer Smallwood (guider), Joan Davies (commissioner), Anita Stevens. *(Stourbridge News Incorporating County Express)*

Wordsley Conservatives Bowling Club, 1925. Back row, left to right: D. Fradgley, Len Loynes, Stan Rowley, Bill Sheriff, A. Williams, George Batten, Joe Jones. Middle row: Jim Nation, Bert Keene, Tom Jones, Charlie Randle, Joe Hill, John Collett, Bill Bache, Luke Hand. Front row: Ted Price, Anthony Bailey, George Sneyd, Bob Hingley, Ben Davies, Jack Hand, Charlie Stanier, Fred Hall. *(Wordsley History Society)*

Wordsley Hospital Cricket Club, 1962. Back row, left to right: V. Shingleton, N. Wilkes (captain), A. Rowbottom, M. Dainty, T. Knott, V. Wood, G. Lord. Front row: -?-, J. Timmins, G. Whiteman, J. Knowles, V. Ellis, G. Knowles. *(Wordsley History Society)*

In the 1970s local councils were under government pressure to cut expenditure, and it seemed that the Audnam Training Centre was under threat. Strong opposition to the possible financial cuts was expressed by the trainees and their supporters. They collected a petition of some 10,000 signatures to present to Dudley Council. This demonstration against the closure of the centre was in April 1979. The centre survived. *(Stourbridge News Incorporating County Express)*

Volunteers at the Mind Charity shop at the bottom of Wordsley High Street, 1978. Mrs V. Petrie is second on the left. *(Stourbridge News Incorporating County Express)*

The Rt Hon. Earl Attlee KG, OM, CH, former leader of the Labour Party, 1935–55, Deputy Prime Minister 1940–5, Prime Minister 1945–51, visited Wordsley on 7 July 1956 to open an extension to the Labour Club in New Street. Here he is seen with a club official, Len Angel. The only other recorded visit to Wordsley by one who had held the office of Prime Minister was when Winston Churchill spoke at the Richardson Hall on 20 January 1906 in support of his cousin, the unsuccessful Liberal candidate in the 1906 General Election. *(Ron Price)*

Dr Bartlett, President of the Women's Branch of Wordsley British Legion, presenting service awards, 1960. Left to right: Edith Jones, S. Baker, Gwen Wale, Dr Bartlett, Victoria Chater. *(Stourbridge News Incorporating County Express)*

At this County British Legion event in 1955, Wordsley British Legion was represented by Edith Jones (front right), Dr Twedell, president (fifth from right), Mrs Twedell (seventh from right) and Mary Chuter (third standard bearer from right, now Mrs J. Skidmore). *(Mrs M. Hayes)*

A group from Wordsley British Legion Ladies Section, 1965. Left to right: Mrs Lockett-Humphries, Edith Jones (secretary), Mary Skidmore, -?-, Gwen Wale, Maud Baker, -?-. *(Stourbridge News Incorporating County Express)*

The Phoenix Centre is an independent local charity which helps children with special needs. In 1972 a group of therapists and volunteers established a playgroup at Kingswinford Youth Centre for children with disabilities in the Dudley Borough. Demand for places was overwhelming and after intensive fund raising a purpose-built centre was established in 1976 on land near Fairhaven Primary School, Wordsley, and extended in 1978. Wordsley was a good source of volunteers, and Dudley Borough Council leased the building land at a peppercorn rent. There is now a centre manager employed by Dudley Social Services Department, supported by three qualified assistants paid for by the supporters' group, assisted by volunteers, ensuring that each child receives as much individual attention as possible. Here children are dressed as the Seven Dwarves in preparation for the Wordsley Carnival. *(The Phoenix Centre)*

Phoenix Mobile Toy Library was founded in 1973, initially borrowing the Phoenix Playgroup mini-bus. It is believed that it was the first such group in the country to operate this kind of specialist toy library. There are now two covering the Dudley Borough. In 1980 a £6,000 van was given to the group by the Spinning Wheel Road Show, a group of entertainers based in Kidderminster and Bromsgrove. When West Bromwich Albion footballers visited the group they donated an autographed ball to be raffled for funds. The chairman at the time, Margaret Taylor, is seen here. Both the toy library and the playgroup are still independent charities and there remains a continuing demand for their services. *(Stourbridge News Incorporating County Express)*

The growing threat from Hitler's Germany caused the government in February 1939 to announce that in London and principal cities steel air-raid shelters, known as Anderson shelters, would be distributed. These consisted of easily assembled steel sections measuring 6ft 6in by 4ft 6in that could be erected in the garden. They were free to families earning less than £250 p.a. (the average wage at that time was about £150 p.a.) and extra panels were available for large families. By April 1939 280,000 had been delivered and 80,000 a week were being made. In 1939 residents of Stewkins, Wordsley, collaborated to build a communal air-raid shelter in a sand pit between Stewkins and Junction Road. The ladies in the foreground are Mrs Careless and Mrs Smith. *(Gerald Potter)*

Work on the Anderson shelter is well in hand. On the back row, left to right: Peter Hathway, Derek Careless, Muriel Potter (who became a district nurse and midwife), Dorothy Hathway and Gerald Potter standing on the sandbags. Front row: Mrs Careless, Mrs Smith, -?-, Derek Smith. *(Gerald Potter)*

8

People

Anthony Bailey was born in London on 8 March 1872. After his father got a job at Wordsley Brewery in 1886 he was also employed there. After ten years he left to start his own business and in 1906 bought the Wordsley Brewery, which had failed. He converted a building on the road frontage to a cinema, which opened to a programme of films and variety items on 23 December 1912. Eventually he sold the premises to Cecil Couper in March 1923.

In the mid-1900s Anthony lived next to the Peacock Inn at 2 Kinver Street where he was able to indulge his passion for bee keeping. He was a Staffordshire County Councillor from 1925 to 1928, a founder member and president, in 1925, of Wordsley Conservative Club, and the last living member of Kingswinford Court Leet. Anthony was a member of several local history societies. He died in October 1950 aged 78. *(Wordsley History Society)*

Joseph Arthur Bradley, born in 1899, became headmaster of Audnam Senior School, George Street, in 1939. His grandfather and father had both been foreman bricklayers at Round Oak Steelworks. Arthur was educated at Bent Street School, Brierley Hill, King Edward VI School, Stourbridge, and entered Birmingham University aged 17 to study Physics.

Once 18 he registered for military service, but because of defective eyesight was passed only for garrison duties. Wanting to be more useful technically, he and several other students registered for an intensive wireless telegraphy course and obtained the Postmaster General's Certificate qualifying him to operate telegraphy apparatus as a first-class operator on British ships. There followed war-related voyages conveying troops, wounded servicemen, hospital patients and nursing staff on several ships with calls at many ports between Gibraltar and Hong Kong. He finally signed off in April 1919 and returned to university, graduating in 1922, following with a teaching diploma the next year. His teaching career included service at Bromley School, Bent Street Boys' School, the new Brierley Hill Intermediate School, back to Bent Street as headmaster and then to Audnam School. He retired in 1960 and died in 1984. *(John Bradley)*

Dudley-born John Collett was recruited from St Paul's Training College for Teachers, Cheltenham, by the Wordsley curate, the Revd A.G. Girdlestone (who was deputising for his father the Revd Charles Girdlestone, the Rector, who lived at Weston-super-Mare), to succeed Benjamin Johnson, headmaster of the National School, from 1 January 1877. Collett married Fanny Holmes of Junction House and they settled at Rose Cottage, 1 New Street, Wordsley, and had two daughters and two sons.

During his forty-four years as headmaster he held many church and civic offices: secretary of the Parochial Church Council, Sunday School superintendent for forty years, Kingswinford Rural District Councillor from 1917 to 1929, member of Stourbridge Board of Guardians, Stourbridge and District Water Board, chairman of Wordsley and District Allotment Holders' Association, treasurer of Wordsley Carnival Committee, secretary of the War Memorial Committee and president of the area branch of the National Union of Teachers. He died on 6 May 1931 and is buried in Wordsley churchyard. *(Author's Collection)*

Christopher J.E.G. Firmstone was born in Wall Heath but spent much of his childhood at Wordsley Manor. The Firmstone family had large coalmining and iron making interests in the Black Country throughout the nineteenth and twentieth centuries. After attending Bromsgrove School, Christopher studied at the Birmingham School of Architecture, qualifying in 1960. After gaining experience with a Birmingham practice he set up on his own in 1964 and soon specialised in the design of art and historical exhibitions. These included work at the National Portrait Gallery, Tate Gallery and the Royal Academy of Arts. He was also responsible for the Victoria & Albert Museum's first Twentieth-Century Primary Gallery and the restoration and adaptation of the Strand Block for the Courtauld Galleries, 1981–92. Between 1991 and 1992 he designed the Visitor Centre for the Elgar Foundation in Worcestershire. Christopher returned to the Black Country in 1992 on inheriting Wordsley Manor, the fifth generation of Firmstones to own the house. Since then he has concentrated on restoring the property and consultancy work. In addition he spends much time painting and has held many exhibitions of his work in London and the West Midlands. (Christopher Firmstone)

Robert Gregg was Audnam School's most outstanding footballer. In the 1952/3 season, after trial matches, he was selected to play for the Brierley Hill, Sedgley & Tipton Area XI, and in each of the first seven matches he scored a hat-trick. His record was 39 goals in 17 games, including 9 hat-tricks. This record earned him a place in the Birmingham County XI and for England Schoolboys v Wales at Cardiff in which he scored two goals in England's 4–2 victory. A coach party from Audnam School travelled to Cardiff to support him. After leaving school he joined Middlesbrough Football Club. (Author's Collection)

Guy Grindlay was born in Jersey on 11 November 1866, educated in Edinburgh and studied medicine there, qualifying as a doctor in 1889. After a year as a ship's doctor he joined Dr Edwin Taylor at a practice in Audnam, which is still doctors' premises (Three Villages Practice). On the death of Dr Turner, Grindlay took over the practice. He also served as the Medical Officer of Health to Kingswinford Rural District Council for over thirty years, MO to the Isolation Hospital in Stallings Lane and also to the Poor Law Institution (Wordsley Workhouse) and as Kingswinford's Public Vaccinator.

Outside medicine Dr Grindlay was also a Director of Harper & Moore Ltd, brickmakers at Colley Gate, becoming chairman in 1930, and he also played golf. According to the *County Express*, some 2,000 people attended his funeral in May 1930. He left a son, Robert Walter Guy Grindlay. *(H. Jack Haden)*

Harry Jack Haden was born at Ivydene, John Street, Wordsley, on 28 June 1916 and educated at nearby Brook Street School, and King Edward VI School, Stourbridge. At 18 he became an indentured editorial apprentice on the *County Express*. Over the next fifty years, as a reporter, he covered every sort of activity in the Stour Valley. His family's glass manufacturing background and his profession gave him the impetus to study the history of the local glass industry in depth, on which he is an acknowledged international expert. For six years, from April 1940, this unassuming man was a private in the Royal Army Medical Corps, landing in Normandy on D + 19, his unit following the front line through to Schleswig-Holstein, and experiencing the full horrors of the Second World War. Back at the *County Express* he became chief reporter, a position he held, despite offers of advancement until he retired in 1985. In retirement he contributed articles for the *Dictionary of National Biography* and is an active member of a number of societies. *(H. Jack Haden)*

Albert Hall was born in Wordsley in 1882. He played for Stourbridge Football Club in 1903 and in the same year was bought by Aston Villa. An outside left, he formed an effective partnership with Joe Bache who had signed for the Villa from Stourbridge in 1901. Albert played in every round when the Villa won the FA Cup in 1905. He and Bache played for England against Ireland in 1913. He joined Millwall in 1913 and retired in 1916. While serving with the South Staffs during the First World War he was badly gassed, and consequently he suffered from ill health for the rest of his life. After the war he became an enamel manufacturer. He died aged 75 on 17 October 1957. (*Patrick Talbot*)

Charles Hatton was born in 1905, the son of E.W. Hatton, Headmaster of Wordsley Church of England School. After attending King Edward VI School, Stourbridge, he became a bank clerk. He wrote and produced for Wordsley Amateur Dramatic Society and from 1932 was a freelance writer. He married in 1942 and moved to Kent in 1949. He contributed articles to a wide variety of paying outlets including collaborations with Francis Durbridge ('Paul Temple') and Ted Willis ('Dixon of Dock Green'). Over fifty years his output of novels, plays, radio scripts and press articles probably made him Wordsley's most prolific writer. He died in Orpington in 1972. (*H. Jack Haden*)

Geoff Hill of Lawnswood was an electrical goods retailer in Brettell Lane from 1958. His business became one of the top independents in the country. In 1989 it moved to High Street, Amblecote. His pre-business career was very varied: British Under 18 Cycling Champion, wartime 'Bevin Boy', commercial traveller, contract caterer, pub landlord, fancy goods wholesaler. His charitable work is legendary. At Mary Stevens Hospice, Stourbridge he helped to raise over £2 million (Hospice Lottery and charity shops). Ten per cent of the profits of his business go to the Geoff Hill Charitable Trust, which has distributed £100,000 to 300 worthy causes in the district. In June 2004 he was awarded the MBE in the Queen's Birthday Honours List. (*Geoff Hill MBE*)

Don Kenyon was born in Alwen Street, Wordsley, on 15 May 1924, attended Brook Street School, Audnam School (where headmaster, Fred Dale, a former Minor Counties cricketer gave him coaching), and Brierley Hill School of Commerce. He joined Stourbridge Cricket Club and made his debut for the 1st XI in 1939. A volunteer for the RAF in 1942, he was able to play cricket regularly for representative sides. In August 1946 he scored 107 in two hours for the RAF against Worcestershire. This led to a Worcestershire County contract and the next twenty-one years were ones of continuous progress and record breaking. He became captain of the county side in 1959 and led the team to the County Championships in 1964 and 1965. He was selected eight times for England and retired from cricket in 1967 with a Worcestershire record of 34,490 runs. An England selector for six years, he became Worcestershire County Cricket Club president in 1986. He died on 12 November 1996 during a visit to County Headquarters. *(Author's Collection)*

Benjamin Frank Mason was born in 1860 and attended Holly Hall School, where he progressed to pupil teacher and qualified as a teacher at the Worcester Diocesan Training College, Saltley, Birmingham, in August 1878. He taught in Birmingham for a short period before being appointed second master at a Brierley Hill School. After three years he became head of Wordsley Board School, which was established in the Wesleyan Methodist Church at Brettell Lane. When new premises were built at Brook Street, Wordsley, in 1884, his position was confirmed. He went to live in Wollaston in 1885 and participated in church affairs as a warden of St James's Church and in civic affairs as an independent councillor on Stourbridge Council from 1910 until his death on 5 August 1925. During the First World War he served with the Worcestershire Volunteers from October 1914 until May 1919. In Wordsley he was joint secretary of the Building Committee and a leading campaigner for the provision of a School of Art. *(Author's Collection)*

On leaving school John Massey took charge of Ashwood Nurseries, which his father had bought on impulse. He intended to move on after a year, but has been there ever since. His high standing in the world of horticulture has been achieved by working in the job day by day for over forty years. Since Ashwood's first Royal Horticultural Society's display in 1991, which won a gold medal, over thirty gold medals have been won. In 2003 John was awarded the RHS's prestigious Gold Veitch Memorial Medal in recognition of 'his contribution to the advancement and improvement of the science of horticulture'. The nursery is much involved in plant breeding and the production of seeds, and a large proportion of plants on sale are grown on the 15-acre site. In addition, a large garden supplies shop, a well-stocked gift shop and a 100-seater refreshment room make Ashwood Nurseries, set astride an historic site, a most attractive place to visit. *(John Massey)*

Philip Pargeter was born in Wordsley on 13 February 1826 and died on 19 December 1906. He trained under Benjamin Richardson, his uncle, in all aspects of glass manufacture, specialising in engraving. He ran his own business at Audnam for eleven years before entering into a partnership with W.S. Hodgetts and his uncle. The partnership was dissolved in 1871 and Philip took over the Red House Glassworks. It was under his direction that a blank of the famous Portland Vase was produced for his cousin John Northwood to decorate. The secrets of the ancient artists had been penetrated, and this led to a revival of a long-lost art, cameo glassmaking. Philip was a public-spirited man, serving as chairman of the Board of Guardians, and for a period on the early Staffordshire County Council. On moving to Stourbridge he served on the early Urban District Council, and on Worcestershire County Council. He was also a magistrate. In 1882 he sold the Red House to Frederick Stuart who had been a partner at the adjacent Albert Glassworks in Bridge Street. *(H. Jack Haden)*

George Philpott, a skilled engineering craftsman who was a forge and die shop superintendent, came to Wordsley in 1966. He was typical of that band of twentieth-century middle management who had progressed from the shop floor to posts of responsibility and collectively formed the backbone of Black Country industry. With only one daughter of their own, George and his wife Kath have always had an extended family, for from 1960 to 1982, they fostered thirty-four children, usually for up to twelve months. Of this number, two boys and one girl became permanent family members. For several years George was chairman of Dudley Social Services Foster Parents' Association. From 1951 to 1993 he acted with Bank Street Methodist Church Dramatic Society, and after retiring from there developed a solo act as a raconteur, donating his fees to charity. For many years he sang with Amblecote Singers, of which he was Chairman for twelve years, and later with Cradley Male Voice Choir. He was a long-time member of Brierley Hill Physically Handicapped Club and was on the committee. *(Author's Collection)*

Barry Randle, Wordsley-born (1942) newsagent, took up motorcycle racing after being a member of Audnam Wheelers Cycling Club. His first machine was a Francis Barnett 197cc that was followed by a succession of more powerful machines, which led him to club racing and then short circuit racing. His first race was at Thruxton Aerodrome in 1961. He was a 'privateer' paying all his own expenses, and at Oulton Park in 1963 recorded his first victory. He achieved firsts and placings at Castle Combe, and in 1963 took part in the Isle of Man TT events. In 1970 Reg Gower, then owner of a DIY supplies shop in Brettell Lane, supplied Barry with a Yamaha 250cc machine, on which he came second in 1971 to Phil Read, former World Champion in the TT, at 95.87 mph. In the Italian Monza Grand Prix in September 1971 he finished third, reaching speeds of 116 mph. On several occasions Barry was just beaten by Mike Hailwood, Giacomo Agostini and Brian Ball. He just lacked that touch of good fortune and big-time sponsorship which would have taken him to the top. *(Author's Collection)*

L.J. (Jack) Roberts joined the staff of Audnam Secondary School in 1950. Called up for the RAF in 1943, he flew in Dakotas in South-East Asia. On demobilisation he trained as a teacher, specialising in art. At the school he will be remembered for his spectacular back-cloths for the annual operetta productions and his interest in school sports. When the school moved to Buckpool he was appointed head of the art department. For several years he was leader of Wordsley Boys' Club at Wordsley Community Centre. The photograph shows him at his retirement party in 1985 after teaching Wordsley pupils for thirty-five years. *(L.J. Roberts)*

Dr William Tweddell (1897–1985) was born of farming stock in Whickham, Co. Durham, and joined the Army on leaving school. He was commissioned in the Durham Light Infantry and by May 1917 had won the MC and Bar at Passchendaele. He was demobbed as a lieutenant and went to Aberdeen University to study medicine. From the age of seven he played golf on a nine-hole course that ran across his father's farm, and by the time he joined the Army was already up to scratch. At university he became a star player. After qualifying as a doctor he served in hospitals in Aberdeen and Oldham before settling in to general practice in Wordsley. Here his golfing achievements included British Amateur Golf Championship (1927), Midland Open (1927), Worcestershire Amateur Championship (1928, 1929, 1931), Great Britain and Ireland Walker Cup (playing captain 1928, non-playing captain 1936), Royal and Ancient Golf Club (captain 1961–2), captain of Stourbridge Golf Club (1928), president of Stourbridge Golf Club (1955–7). He continued to play into his seventies. *(Mrs M. Hayes)*

Johann van Leerzem's father was a chief petty officer in the Royal Dutch Navy, who came to Britain during the Second World War and settled in Wolverhampton after marrying a local girl. Johann came to live in Wordsley when he became an inspector for Stourbridge and District Water Board. In 1982 he became regulation's inspector for the South Staffordshire Waterworks Company, where he became interested in the firm's history and had access to their records. Soon he was able to contribute to the company's in-house magazine, arrange exhibitions of photographs and documents and write the company history. This encouraged him to join a Wolverhampton Polytechnic (University from 1992) course leading to a degree. His studies were progressing well when he suffered renal failure. Despite hospital dialysis treatment three days a week he was able to complete his thesis and was awarded a Master of Philosophy degree in autumn 2000. He was a true scholar and a self-taught researcher who left school without any qualifications, but pursued his interest in the history of water supply to a high level. He died on 13 January 2003, aged 57. *(Author's Collection)*

Fred Willetts was born in 1919 at 15 Belle Vue, Wordsley. He attended Lawnswood School from the age of five and at eight transferred to the National (Church) School, leaving in 1933 when he became a gardener. He joined Wordsley Hospital gardening team in 1941 and became head gardener in 1954. After a reorganisation at the hospital he worked elsewhere for a time before returning as head porter for a spell. He married a hospital sister in 1946 and their daughter was born in 1948. A widower since 1987, he and a former schoolfriend, the late Bert Rowbottom, founded Wordsley History Society and built up an impressive collection of old photographs and slides of the district. He is now president of this society. *(Black Country Bugle)*

Jim Worton, born in Brierley Hill in 1907, christened James Edmund Valentine Worton, was educated there and at King Edward VI School, Stourbridge. He was a fellow pupil of Noel Brettell, poet and writer, and of Ernie Quinton, teacher and local historian. On leaving school in 1923 he became an apprentice hairdresser in Brierley Hill, had a short spell at Round Oak Steelworks and then joined Mrs Crossley's hairdressing business in Brettell Lane. After his marriage in 1930 he opened his own hairdresser's at 145 Brettell Lane, bought the property in 1955 and worked until 1978 and part-time afterwards until 1983. This 1960s photograph shows 'Sweeney Todd' Jim in action on Jimmy Painter, a retired baker, then 80 years old, in the chair. A keen gardener, he had an allotment behind Oakfield (Hawbush) Community Centre and was a main prize winner on several occasions in the Dudley Borough competition. *(Trevor Worton)*

J. Trevor Worton, born in 1935, missed much schooling because of a childhood illness. On leaving Audnam School in 1950 he joined his father's hairdressing business. In order to do his National Service in the RAF he signed on for three years and became a driver of the Queen Mary 60 long vehicles used for the transport of aircraft by road. During a Midlands assignment with four colleagues with four such vehicles he brought them to Brettell Lane where they all parked and caused a traffic jam. When demobbed he turned down a job as an HGV driver, choosing to joined his father's business. He continued as a hairdresser until 2003 when ill health forced him to retire. *(Trevor Worton)*

George Yardley came from Black Country stock. His father sought work in South Wales where George was born in 1915, and then Yorkshire. George was educated at Doncaster Grammar School. Employment prospects were poor, so he joined the Army. He passed out from Catterick Camp in 1935 as a Wireless & Line Operator and was posted to India in 1937 as signaller in the Royal Corps of Signals. He volunteered for the First Indian Parachute Brigade and in 1944 was commissioned lieutenant. On his return to Britain in 1944 he was promoted to captain and served at Whitby until demobilisation. After the war he trained as a teacher and started at Brook Street Primary School on 1 November 1950. He worked his way up, becoming deputy headmaster, and for the last year of his service headmaster, retiring in 1980. He had a large range of sporting interests and was an active official in area sports activities, including the successful Brierley Hill, Sedgley and Tipton Schools Football Association. He was also a qualified youth leader. He died in 2000. *(Mrs L. Yardley)*

9

West of Wordsley

Tinker's Cottage on the Prestwood Road was built by the Canadian-born architect Major Kenneth Hutchinson Smith, who settled in the Midlands after serving in the First World War. He built the house in 1934 for a well-known shoe retailer, Mr B. Collins, using part of the original cottage on the site. The Major's method of construction for the fifty-plus properties he built has been described as 'genuine mock Tudor' and 'the most honest fakes in the business'. He stuck rigidly to the methods of medieval master builders and used materials from derelict timbered houses for which he scoured the Welsh border country. Originally thatched, this house was re-roofed with tiles after a fire in 1951. During the Second World War it was used as a retreat for US officers. It is now the home of local businessman Geoff Hill. *(Author's Collection)*

Hunter's Lodge II was built by George Wood, a builder of twenty years, who had been fired with a dream to build a medieval manor house. With an overdraft on the original house on the site, he could not afford to buy another piece of land. His answer was to demolish his original house and build his dream house in its place. This he did, and he and his son Marcus lived under polythene on the site as gradually Hunter's Lodge II took shape. The same skills used by medieval craftsmen, and revived by Major Kenneth Hutchinson Smith in the Midlands between 1924 and 1940, were used here by George Wood. They have produced a magnificent construction which is pure Hutchinson Smith, writ large and true. *(Author's Collection)*

Ashwood Pumping Station was built after successful boreholes were sunk in the Greenforge area, which proved that a plentiful supply of good-quality water existed in the sandstone bedrock. The Earl of Dudley was a prime mover in the matter. Boring operations on the site started soon after the 1888 tests and the engine/pump house and chimney stack were completed in October 1892. Eventually there were six boreholes varying in depth from 286ft to 621ft, sunk into the Bunter sandstone, which produced 4 million gallons a day. Coal was brought to Ashwood Wharf and then by horse and cart to the station to work the pump. Connection to the public supply started in July 1893. Cottages for workers were built nearby. Electrification of the plant commenced in 1958. This view shows the station as it is today. *(Author's Collection)*

The eighteenth-century bridge across Ashwood Basin, early twentieth century. It is still an important link between Wordsley and the west, although now only in single lane use. (*Author's Collection*)

Greensforge lay on the Roman road linking the salt settlement of Droitwich with Uxacona (near Oakengates) on Watling Street. For a short period in the first century, after AD 47, Greensforge and the roads emanating from it were of strategic significance. After this the frontier moved further west and this area became more settled with the Roman occupation. *Key to aerial photograph:* 1. Ashwood Nurseries; 2. Ashwood Marina; 3. Mile Flat; 4. Dawley Brook; 5. Navigation Inn; 6. Staffs/Worcs Canal; 7. Smestow Brook; 8. Hinksford; 9. Wombourne; 10. Swindon; 11. Camp farm; Fort A; 12. Roman Road/Droitwich; 13. Roman Road to Pennocrucium; Fort B; 14. Roman Road to Bridgnorth a, b and c marching camps; d and e marching camps to the west. (*Ashwood Nurseries*)

Prestwood House, south-west elevation, once in the Parish of Kingswinford, was situated just off the present A449 near to the former Stewponey Hotel. The Prestwood Estate sale catalogue of July 1913 states that the property had been in the Foley family since 1650. It was once a hunting lodge in the Kinver Forest, the keeper of which resided in Stourton Castle. Other families associated with the house included the Dudleys, Littletons, Sebrights and Hodgsons. 'Red' Humphrey Littleton hid at Prestwood, his old home, after he was found to have hidden Gunpowder Plot conspirators Robert Winter and Stephen Littleton at his home at Hagley Hall.

A house was built here by Sir John Littleton in Elizabethan times on the site of John de Somery's original dwelling. This was demolished in 1766 and replaced with one modelled in Gothic style, which was stuccoed in 1821. In the mid-1920s it was bought as a hospital for chest diseases, but during alterations a fire broke out and it had to be demolished. A new hospital was built on the site, which is now a nursing home. *(Angus Dunphy)*

Prestwood House, south-east elevation. The ground floor had nine large rooms in addition to the usual range of support buildings, including laundry, brewhouse, bakery, game larder, bottle store, coal store and dog kennels. On the first floor there were ten principal bed and dressing rooms and on the second floor another ten bed and dressing rooms. The domestic offices were extensive and included a spacious kitchen, scullery, larder, dairy, servants' hall, housemaids' room, boot, lamp and knife rooms, butler's sitting room and pantry. *(Angus Dunphy)*